Nissim Ezekiel:
Poetry as Social Criticism

Nissim Ezekiel: Poetry as Social Criticism

Qamar Talat
A.A. Khan

ADHYAYAN

ADHYAYAN PUBLISHERS & DISTRIBUTORS
New Delhi-110 002

Published by
ADHYAYAN PUBLISHERS & DISTRIBUTORS
4378/4B, 105, J.M.D. House, Murari Lal Street
Ansari Road Darya Ganj, New Delhi - 110002
Ph.: 011-23263018, 011-23277156, Fax: 011-23280028
Email: adhyayanpublishers@yahoo.com

Nissim Ezekiel: Poetry as Social Criticism

Edition 2009
ISBN 978-81-8435-160-6

Printed in India

Published by Harish Chandra Yadav for Adhyayan Publishers & Distributors, Delhi. Laser Typesetting at Spectrum Media, Daryaganj and Printed at Tarun Offset Printers, Delhi

Acknowledgements

I feel a great pleasure in stating that I personally contacted Nissim Ezekiel in the year 1985-86. He profoundly encouraged me by way of discussing about poetry in general, and his own poetry in particular, by way of sparing one precious hour. Then and their, I made up my mind to make an analytical study of his poetry. I herewith acknowledge the profound encouragement that he gave me on the occasion. There onwards, on innumerable occasion he enlightened me on the delicate point of appreciating poetry through innumerable letters he wrote to me.

I am thankful to my publisher Shri Harish Chandra Yadav. It is due to him that my work saw light of the day.

Durg

25-06-09

Qamar Talat

A.A. Khan

Preface

Nissim Ezekiel's poetry is informed by his criticism. His criticism is characterised by the smugness of Indian culture as he found it; and his poetry and criticism both culminate into a great human document in his poetry. In the essay 'Naipaul's India and Mine' he harshly exposes Naipaul's attitude towards India and its present. Ezekiel honestly suggests that the Indian situation needs creative criticism and sympathetic reformation rather than inhuman better-than-thou egotistical exposures. Says Ezekiel 'I see India in most ways as Naipaul sees' (Yes, I see her sick). All that he says against the grossness and speller of Indian life, the routine ritualism, the lip-service to high ideals, the patricide and distorted sense of clearness and a thousand other things, all this is true. My dissatisfaction is with his mode of argument, his false examples. If so Ezekiel's poetic commitments are very clear.

In critically exposing India and its cultural milieu, he adopts for himself a rare poetical 'mode of argument', by way of avoiding the false examples. The poetry of Ezekiel is a vast criticism of life, not only India but also of the entire humanity. As a poet and critic his honest commitment goes with 'the caricature and mockery' of all that is human (to borrow his own phrase), while in attacking V.S. Naipaul, in the same essay, Ezekiel exposes the foul ideals of life embraced by the Indians. The failures of Indians go deep into its history An average Indian is not ready to believe that his failure is due to his ideals he attributes, his failure do not live up to this ideals. So the contradiction between words and behaviour which is universal turns into an insensitive contradiction between belief and the way of life. It is this way of life that Ezekiel exposes in his poetry without condescending to satirical malignity.

Nissim Ezekiel in a very casual and in pack-sniff manner humorously exposes from astrology to palmistry; star-gazing to face reading; from yoga to *churna;* herbs and leaves to stone and gems; *tantras, yantras, mantras* and music; metals and beads; colours and fragrances; potions for health lotions for pain and concoctions for the palate all such fooling concoctions with which the Indians deceive their fellowmen, without any pain or feeling in their conscious. Almost every thing that shrouds this land and its people in mystery and ignorance is on show in his poetry. The veil may not be eventually lifted through all the sensible efforts to rationalise the Indian masses. However, it is a matter of great bafflement as to how India lives in ten centuries simultaneously. It is this contingent manner in which the Indian masses live their lives that interest Nissim Ezekiel as a poet and invokes him sympathetically to expose the foolish manner of the public as a sincere fellowman bent upon reforming the ignorant masses.

Much of the Indian writing in English is palpable in design and bluffing in purpose. The Indian writer starts with an idea of offering a message or a lesson to the rest of the world about India and its rich heritage. Hence, we can call this a motivated and purposive writing, which goes near to vain propaganda rather than touching the base of artistic creation. It is altogether a different matter to write about the regional specialities and to make an inflated slogan on behalf of the regional, sentimentalities. Most of the poets and writers indulge in a sort of sentimental praise of India or they criticize Indianness harshly. Nissim Ezekiel is an exception here. But he pays a greater attention to how he says, leaving aside what he says to be imaginatively recaptured by the readers. This is so at least in his poetry, if not in all his other writings. He is doubtfully fortunate in catching the verse and potentially of 'free verse' and the traditional metrical patterns. He has personal liking for modern experimental writing through honest introspection. Ezekiel's poetry is what it gives a living literary form and spirit for his poetry.

With the above intention in mind I propose to make in-deep analysis of Ezekiel's poetry. My main aim is to bring out his lucid critical intentions into a sort of togetherness in his poetry. More than anything else the modern existential preoccupations and the phenonial prot cesses of a creative mind enchanted him most. An attempt is made to elucidate his existential agonies and perceptions profundities of beauty around him, with a rare purpose of enhancing the human understanding of nature, fellowmen, and all the predicaments of life of man in the urban scenario of modern times.

The book is divided into Six Chapters, with an Introduction.

In writing this work, I have closely followed the *MLA Style Sheet* in citing the notes and the references, as well as in preparing the Bibliography. The illustrations of Ezekiel's poems are mostly taken from *Journal of South Asian Literature.* Whenever, the quotations are taken from his other poetical collections, the references are promptly recorded likewise. The main interest of my work lies in the appreciatory explications of individual poems. An attempt is also made to capture the exact intentionalities and commitments of Nissim Ezekiel.

Contents

1
Introduction

Nissim Ezekiel looks upon both the European and instant tradition from the point of view of new humanism that started during 1890s. At the time, he observes contemporary institutions and cultures from the point of view of tradition. The resultant essence of his poetry, the glorious criticism, old as well as new conventions of life of our times. As a critic of life and morals, he always hoped for a new sensibility and new awareness in the process of appreciating life's delicated dimensions.

Nissim Ezekiel is a post-Independence Indo-Anglian poet. Progressively publishing his short poems from time to time since 1952 till today. After 1947 a new India was born with its new institutions, new hopes and new ways of approach. The ideas of democracy, secularism and unity in diversity are the most important and urgent social innovations which needed a new clarity of approach. Ezekiel aims at poetically establishing the personal ways of arriving at the new clarity. To that extent, poetry for Ezekiel is a medium of personal experience. All these new institutional properties needed a tender care; and Ezekiel's poetry maintains that tenderness of approach towards these institutions.

many languages and poetry was written in those languages and in Sanskrit, the universal mother of all languages. But, however with all the greatness of these poetries, it can be said that there was no single poetical movement which touched all the Indian languages in a unified manner. There were certainly competitive and self-contained poetic movements in various parts of India, during various times, all with various dimensional importance. As a result, we had Bengali poetry, Marathi poetry, Punjabi poetry, Telugu poetry and Urdu poetry flourishing variously in various times at various places. If at all there was any unity in the whole creative atmosphere of India, it was there in the glorious Vedic traditions, the spirit of which was continuously maintained in almost all the local languages. The credit for this goes to Sanskrit and Prakrit as universal languages affecting the whole of India. During the Mughal Regime Arabic and Persian also contributed for the development of a homogeneous poetic spirit in the different Indian languages. It was the introduction of English into the Indian universities that could suddenly open up new vistas of humanism, which can be categorically considered as Western humanism inherited from ancient Greek and Romans and synthesized by Christainity. This, in particular, touched all the parts of India with intensity and vigour. The salient features of Western humanism will be elaborated. The concept of Indian poetry could be possibly experimented after the English touched the parts of India. As a result, we have plenty of Indian poetry independently practised and propagated through English. Thus, we have that *Indo-Anglian-poetic-movement.* For its largeness of appeal and for its synthetic homogeneity Indo-Anglian poetry deserves a place of pride. Ezekiel, as a mouthpiece of this movement, establishes for himself a commendable claim and place, as an original creative writer of poetry in English in India.

Nissim Ezekiel is a romantic idealist nurturing in himself innumerable dreams for a free and felicitous India. However, it is worth noting that romanticism as a poetic movement died its natural death after W.B. Yeats and a few other British poets. Thereby Ezekiel, when he particularly stressed on the old romantic ideals, looks slightly outlandish and even decadent, not condescending however, to the decadent poetic purposes of the Georgian poets. At the same time, he inherits the immediate Western naturalist-realist traditions through education and culture. As a result, he develops a tone of defiance and non-confornism extending to skeptical dimensions. Hopelessness, depravity and loss of faith are their everywhere for him to see; but, however, through his poetic endeavour he always wanted to arrive at 'a bold nectarean answer for the poison of the present' (to borrow the expression of K.R.S. Iyengar). His great search for nectarean answer always hastened him towards maintaining hopeful deductions from out of what he experienced as a hopeless performance in operation. It is here that his authentic self falls at its either or dilemma; and thereby, the division of his soul is their to see for everbody. But, however one thing that consolidates his poetic stand is to be found in the unifiedness of his personal experiences which ultimately go to take his analogical poetic forms. The apparent dilemma gets resolved in the uniqueness of his personal experiences. Ezekiel's poetry (to borrow the expression of W. Stevens) 'is a medium of personal experience', and the uniqueness of this 'personal' temper of temperament is found in Ezekiel's poetry.

Nissim Ezekiel's personal poetry has a profound social purpose. As a poet he takes upon himself the fine art of telling people what all he considers to be an ideal process of human experience in a given situation. He is a bitter critic of traditional institutions. But, at the same time, he realizes the utter inevitable need of these institutions for the well-being of man. As such he always wanted to reform the attitudes of the people towards the life giving institutions. For that purpose, democracy, modern India, secularism and humanism are the glorious institutional essences to which he addresses himself as a fond lover and concerned critic. It is this quality of Ezekiel that wins him substantial place as a poet-thinker. It is with this thinker's attitude that he looks at what may be called the new Indian experience.

Ezekiel's ultimate concern is with India and its various ethnic groups that live in it. The traditional India, according to him, is always back-looking and primitive. To turn the huge Indian masses towards an achievable unified future, he hastens to attack the evils in very bitter tones, if necessary, and clarifies the visions of the people towards a par-excellent human India. India is a land of innumerable cultures, languages and ethnic codes of conduct and behaviour. The only factor that unifies India quite ironically of course is its poverty. This poverty includes economical poverty and poverty of understanding. Ezekiel aimed at poetically dealing the people against the dangers of poverty, ignorance and irresponsible manners of existence. According to Ezekiel, life has to be lived in perfect freedom of understanding in a depth analytical manner. He satirically denounces all inauthentic, superficial purposes serving styles of life. His ultimate aim is in creating the sort of human consciousness, free from all kind of inhibitions and taboos. His poetic attempt is a sort of pathological operation on the vision of people. To that extent, he assumes upon himself the stylistic nuances of doctor in operation. Writing poetry in the present context any where in the world, is not a pleasant job. The world's great aestheticians started addressing themselves towards the bitter social realities. Ezekiel takes up the same task and continues to write poetry on the same line.

In addressing himself to the Indian masses, Ezekiel always maintains a sort of poetical view towards the global human situations. His Indianism is a more poetic address to the entire humanity. His poetry is essentially an individual appeal. At the same time, it is a great clarifier of the very stands and projects of a never-ending, ever continuous process in operation. For this operation adjudication standards are exclusively prompted by the person within or the person's authentic self. With this amount of personal evocative touch Ezekiel wants to establish a new human order where their will not be any inter-personal humiliations. The new human order of Ezekiel is informed by a sense of freedom and intimated by the liberty of imagination; his liberty of imagination in its turn gets informed by pure humanism. In the practical world of Ezekiel, life should by easy, livable and enjoyable in all its proportions and dimensions. In this context, he does not plead for the prevalence or otherwise of the politicalisms. His whole purpose is happy living, good thinking and mutual trust in society. If so, Ezekiel's dream-land is a long way ahead.

In fact, Ezekiel developed for himself a real poetic theory in the context of which a sort of free and frank engagement of his imagination in the act of poetic creation. His poetic theory is similar to the poetic theories of the modern Western poets. In a way, it can be said that he borrowed much in the name of poetic theory, from his Western counterparts. But, at the same time, he introduces his own significant idea of creating a poem, as an act of freedom of engagement of his imagination. It becomes necessary to discuss his 'Theory of Imagination' which in its turn is his 'Poetic Theory'.

2
Formative Influences

Towards the beginning of the twentieth century there emerged a new mutation in the cultural advancement of Europe. This new cultural wave is as revolutionary and novel as the Renaissance of the sixteenth-century Europe. This new cultural wave was immensely responsible in establishing a new humanism, coupled with an awakened sense of interpersonal responsibilities. Referring to this new humanism Virginia Woolf wrote in 1924 that:

> *In or about December, 1910, human character changed, in the context of which, all human relation have shifted – those between masters and servants, husbands and wives, parents and children. And when human relations change there is at the same time a change in religion, conduct, politics and literature.*[1]

Because of the geographical compactness of the present-day world, this new humanism instantly reached all the corners of the world. With a fresh re-awakened sense of human responsibilities this cultural mutation influenced all the walks of life of man, including poetry. Under the influence of this new cultural development there emerged altogether a new poetic trend. This new poetic trend consolidated its achievements towards the middle of the twentieth century in India. Innumerable poets took upon themselves all these new poetic trends that were emerging in England and Europe. Nissim Ezekiel is one such poet who continually offered the aesthetic pleasures of this new poetry. Referring to the emergence of this new poetry in India Dr. K.R.S. Iyengar has to say as follows:

> *A global war spread over several years is apt to liquidate a whole generation – the 'middle' generation. And a new generation comes up with a striking individuality of its own, a sharpness in its features, an angularity in its gestures, a tone of defiance (or at least of non-conformity) in its speech, a gleam of hope in its eyes, a new ardour perhaps, and even new rhythms and nuances and acceptabilities speech.*[2]

The new poetry emerged there is bound to be poetry of protest. With an acute sense of protest, Ezekiel is (again to borrow the words of Iyengar):

> *An artist who is willing to take pains, to cultivate reticence, to pursue the profession of poetry with a sense of commitment, . . .*[3]

Therefore, Ezekiel is a poet with a social and cultural purpose. While his purpose broadly remains a matter of poignant awareness of the demands of his personal instincts, including sex and hunger, his main concerns in poetry express an anguish and anxiety as conformed by the existential thinkers. Like all other modern European poets, he nurtures in himself a painful grievance against the de-humanizing forces of urbanization, mechanization, technocratization and civilization. He constantly exposed all these evils, by way of writing his analogical verse patterns comparable to those of W.B. Yeats, W.H. Auden, T.S. Eliot, Stephen Spender, William Macneice, Ted Hughes and all such other modern English poets who made revolt against the old world Ezekiel joined the line of these protesting generation of poets. His poetry, therefore, is intensely critical substantially oppositional and immensely sceptical. Satire and humour are the flesh and blood of his poetry, while the very bone of his poetic approach lies in expressing the existential anguish, coupled with personal agony. Again to borrow the words of Dr. S. Iyengar:

> *The recurring note in Ezekiel's recent poem is the hurt that urban civilization inflicts on modern man, dehumanizing him and subjecting his verities to pollution and devaluation.*[4]

These evils according to Ezekiel are inherited by man through various institutions that held man slavishly subjugated for centuries together. Personally speaking he was often sceptical about any possible remedy for these evils. He is of a strong opinion that,

> *The pattern will remain, unless you break.*
> *It with a sudden jerk.*[5]

Ezekiel constantly tried at creating such a 'jerk' of protest in his poems. Since his main concerns are with the Indian masses, the very fabric and pattern of his poetry ponders deep into the unfortunate manner in which people live their lives with all their ignorances and traditional taboos intact in the subcontinent.

Feel for Fellowman

Indian is a land of innumerable cultures clogging into glorious innovations. When two cultures come into contact through wars or migrations and assimilate themselves into one cultural whole which is superior to both the cultures coming into contact, the resultant superior culture is technically called 'An Innovation' by the sociologists in the twentieth century itself the Western humanism received a revolutionary change of its attitude. Man for the first time started thinking in terms of understanding his fellow-men. It is all a sort of entering into a personal introspection, in order to find for oneself as to how it looks like being the other. Nissim Ezekiel, with his profound Indian background readily accepted the call and created his poetry of great human understanding. In the process of accomodating this new situation of the new humanism, he was required to look into the old patterns of lifestyles, which are to be thrown out as insufficient formulas of life. For this purpose, he attributed for himself a critical attitude of ironically exposing the dogmatic and patterned traditional formulas of life. Thereby, as a poet, he emerged into a critic of life around himself. Referring to the possible Indian content in Indo-English poetry, Ezekiel, in his essay. 'What is Indian in Indo-English Poetry?' says as follows:

> *There is the sensibility that leans towards the Indian in all areas, including that of poetry; there is the sensibility that leans, let us say, in some other direction; and finally there is the sensibility that struggles to maintain a balance, with or without dignity. Each bias or learning has its dangers, from the dogmatic and doctrinnaire to the farcical and clownish.*[6]

It is with this kind of 'that struggle that maintains a balance', between his inborn Indian sensibility and the acquired foreign sensibility that Ezekiel aims at writing his poetry and other creative writings.

Sense of Being in the World

At the same time Ezekiel looks upon the traditional insufficient patterns of life and institutions around him as a concerned critic for whom a total change is an urgent necessity. The very first collection of his poems *A Time to Change* (1952) is in itself suggestive of his urgency. As a critic he looks at the world with an ironic slant, born of his own personal views and values in conflict with the superficial manner of their application by the people around him. Inauthenticity and insincerity to the fundamental laws of life vex him totally. Most charitably nature endowed man with proper sense and sensibility. Ezekiel whole-heartedly agrees with T.S. Eliot that, some how, a 'dissociation of sensibility'[7] occurred in the seventeenth century Europe. It is this dissociation of sensibility of man from his natural sense of being in the world that caused a great harm to humanity. He fervently pleads for a proper union of sense and sensibility, by way of asking people to be satisfied with the essentials of life, benevolently and charitable granted by nature. Says Ezekiel:

> *A bit of land, a woman and a child or two*
> *Accommodated to their needs and changing moods,*
> *Practising a singing and a talking voice is all the creed*
> *a man of God requires.*[8]

The very process of urbanization which led man to a meaningless life of self-centeredness and discrimination has to be thrown out at any cost. It is for the purpose of propagating this simple truth that he practised poetry, and put forth his own sense of being in the world. In order to achieve this purpose he believes that there is a great necessity of correction. Says Ezekiel:

I start again
With secret faults concealed no more.[9]

A new attempt of understanding life in its elemental and instinctive realities must start, if humanity has to be saved. 'All the secret faults' of his own should not be concealed any more. Any such concealment breeds insincerity and inauthenticity, which are born of ignorance and unknowledged. He knows it all well that it is not very easy to achieve a clear vision of life. Ezekiel does not accept defeat in the hands of the sabotaging forces of achieving a clarity of purpose in life. His poetry is a modest attempt at gaining such a clarity of purpose of living like man. All around him he finds a colossal lack of initiative among the people for this human purpose. The clarity of life has to be achieved by way of involving oneself into honest hopes and dreams as a poet. He aims at establishing his poetry a brave new understanding of life, and its purposes. Therefore, says Ezekiel:

The pure invention or the perfect poem,
Precise communication of a thought,
Love reciprocated to a quiver,
Flawless doctrines, certainty of God,
These are merely dreams; but I am human
And must testify to what they mean.[10]

Referring to this existential urgency of Ezekiel, Inder Nath

Kher says:

> *Through the juxtaposition of art and life he envisions a state of harmony between the inner and outer landscapes. Thus, from the existential-esthetic viewpoint, his poetry represents a structure of creative reality in which all the dichotomies of life are encompassed, in which contraries exist side by side, and in which the encountering self seeks resolution from within the tension caused by opposing forces in nature and in the heart of man and woman. This structure of creative reality is an emblem of a continual process which reveals itself through myriad names and forms, relations and themes, ironies and paradoxes, failures and realizations.*[11]

The 'state of harmony' between the inner and the outer landscape is a matter of arriving at an equanimous adjustment between life and art. But, from an over all understanding of Ezekiel's poetry it emerges that he was trying very hard to acthieve a balance between his artistic forms and his lively poetic aspirations. But he is conscious of his limitations when he says:

> *. . .but I am human*
> *And must testify to what they mean.*[12]

In this process of testification life certainly becomes an insoluable riddle; and all his attempts at achieving a balance receive a setback. He himself honestly confesses that life is still a mystery. Therefore, he hastens to add to the above:

> *For consider how I win redemption*
> *In the private country of my mind*

Where the worser part, as Socrates would say,
Presides.[13]

All his poetic attempts are endeavours to penetrate deep into his own mind where 'the worser part resides'. The existence of this 'worser part in the mind', 'is a harass-ment. He presumptuously borrowed it from the most casual utterances of the religionists and fatalists, who start with a presumption that man is a perpetual sinner Born of the Original Sin, and he is fated to suffer the evils of his race. How far Ezekiel is really consciously convinced with this idea is doubtful. He is not a dogmatic religionist. All the myths of religions are critically looked upon by him from the point of view of a humanist thinker and poet. One of the great rewards of literature is that it can help man to reach across the man-made barriers and walls that divide him from his own being. It aims at mitigating the emotional blindness created by the dogmatic creeds and religions. But, as a poet he very often indulges in this kind of self-denouncing formulas celebrating the religious myths, with a purpose to reveal their shallowness. He is certainly not a dogmatic traditionalist. But, still he likes to have the mystery of life kept intact, for without it there is no magic of life at all:

Our lives are centered there. We cannot love
without the idea of love. The feast
Is spread by gods with friendly wings
Who lead us through the myth and maze.[14]

This is the central core of his philosophy of life. It lies in 'the idea of love' for humanity. This 'idea of love' is what nature conferred on man. So the most necessary change that must emerged in humanity must be centralized in this 'idea of love'. Says Ezekiel:

The food I eat
cannot nourish me
unless I love the human face.[15]

His faith in the 'idea of love' makes him critical in all such lifestyles and myths, which do not contribute to the conscious involvement into love of humanity.

The above argument may go to suggest that Ezekiel is a serious philosophical and spiritual poet contending for himself the claim of a teacher. He honestly acknowledges that this great world of God is still a mystery. Life comes into operations as a miracle. Therefore, art too must emerge as prototype of this miracle. He precisely says that the balances achieved between life and art are abundantly accidental and absolutely unpredictable. Man is endorsed with a sort of accidental prerogative of achievement. If he can be certain of his potentiality and achievement he is likely to become equal to God. He admits that man's lot is to stand at dismay and wonder at the works of God, and understand the creative mystery as a miracle. Therefore, he says:

If this is not a miracle
Then I am God.[16]

It is a miracle and therefore he is man. As a man, he is required to make innumerable permutations and combinations for the purpose of achieving the balance between art and life. In the meantime, he fervently pleads for an open-hearted approach towards life, with pure love at the centre of his heart. This alone gives him a poetic fulfilment. Says Ezekiel:

Insight illumination
Secret faults concealed no more.[17]

Ezekiel's poetry, therefore, is a blend of humility with his own sense of creativity. He adopts for himself a very casual conversational mode of winning the confidence of his readers through persuasions, explosively sparkling with an addition of fun and humour through antithesis. Even the most weighty themes of human inter-personal relations and the existential agonies are casually introduced in his poetry. In this art of creation he never adopts for himself 'a better then thou', posture in relation to his readers. Thereby, he acheives the fullest confidence of his readers, by way of turning against himself through frank and fair confessions. In this sense he can as well be considered as a bitter confessional poet exposing himself first, and the whole world after.

Life's Fulfilment and the Creative Process

Ezekiel believes that the real fulfilment of life in our social context comes with a few affections, charities and adjustments. In effect, we have to be humble cherishers of life, without adopting for ourselves any compulsive or mindless pursuits. Says Ezekiel :

And don't tell me
there's any happiness
in being compulsive
or mindless.[18]

If man sub-serviates himself and renders himself to be a slave to ideas and ideologies he alone is to be blamed. There he says:

Its' fantastic
what a slave
a man can be
who has nobody
to oppress him
except himself.[19]

This is to say that a straight raport with life itself makes him capable of engaging himelf with life in a free and frank manner. Any sort of overview or underview of life, which is usually spread over by the dogmatic institutional norms, has always to be avoided. He again states:

Compared to my mind
rocks are reasonable,
clouds are clear.
It makes me mad
but that is how it is.[20]

The dilemma of life must always be solved by way of adopting for oneself straightforward whole-hearted adjustments with the widespread ironies and mysteries of life. He criticizes people for not being able to live their lives in the here and now, without falling upon the past and future through memory and dream fantasy. Life is given and it has to be adjusted by way of inventing for oneself the immediate and readily acceptable solutions. When the existentialists say that life is 'a given', they do not mean to imply that the solutions for problem of life are solved and given. It is 'a given' in the sense that one has to involve into it, with a readiness to love its mysteries also as 'givens'. The solutions have to be arrived at by oneself. These are the 'limits'. In accepting his 'limits' he is free and frank. Hence he can hope to live with the necessary courage to exist.

People suffer for want of this capacity. For such people life is alwavs a problem and crisis of their own making, and they always find themselves in misery. Therefore, states Ezekiel :

> *All want now*
> *is the recognition*
> *of dilemma*
> *and the quickest means*
> *of resolving it within my limits.*[21]

The frank recognition of his 'limits' speaks for his clear headedness. These 'limits' are both external and internal, i.e. social and personal. He does not mean to say that he would limit his poetic performance, forces and limits. Just he would not take the stance of a rebel. That he realizes and accepts the force of these 'limits' is in itself an indication that he is ready to face them. For quite a long time he followed M.N. Roy and his humanism. This led Ezekiel to develop for himself a new human temper or temperament that looks upon the evils and mysteries with a sense of tolerance and good temper. This new humanism has nothing much to do with the American literary movement propogated by Irving Babbitt and Paul Elmer More. The American literary movement was mainly anti-romantic, anti-realist and anti-naturalist. The new humanism of M.N. Roy takes its roots from the sociological angle. Social justice, which was ironically denied to the masses, was insisted upon not as a new social law or conventions, but as a profound personal choice of standing by the democratic principles of the equality and fraternity. This kind of human temper or temperament must first denounce the age-old feudal habits and social distinctions. The resultant humanism is highly charged with a sense in felt obligation to do ones best to the mankind. It is a sort of introspection and revision of the values within oneself. Even at the point of repetition the words of Ezekiel are worth quoting here:

The food I eat
cannot nourish me
unless I love the human face.[22]

At the outset the words of Ezekiel may appear as slightly sentimental tilting towards Whitmanian formula of considering brotherhood of humanity as all important. But it is not mere statement of assertive declaration of a borrowed ideology. It is the 'cry' of the occasion and the same is supported by the following couplet of Ezekiel:

A man withdrawn into himself
may be a man moving forward.[23]

Ezekiel gives utmost importance to man as a prime species in the nature's work of God. Therefore, he attributes a rare dignity and manliness to humanity. In fact, all his poetry is animated with a sense of 'a man moving foreward'. Again 'the moving foreward' of Ezekiel does not have any thing to do with the common human perception of material progress. It has everything to do with a new leap into human good as the only possible alternative for the humans to exist in the world. He wants to denounce all the masks that man is capable of borrowing for himself in order to claim for himself a false dignity and inauthentic propagation of himself. Ezekiel looks even upon himself with a precautious sense of mistrust and disgusts. Therefore, he sincerely confesses:

> *Even as myself, my very own*
> *incontrovertible, unexceptional*
> *self, I feel I am disguised.*[24]

It is this frankness and good temper that makes him realize 'the secret faults concealed no more'. When the secret faults are not concealed the true vision of life emerges from within. From this standpoint, he argues, that instead of rambling in wilderness one should centralize himself in the 'house' that is his own inner self. Most fervently and persuasively, he asks:

> *We who leave the house in April, Lord,*
> *How shall we return?*
> *Debtors to the whore of love,*
> *Corrupted by the things imagined*
> *Through the winter nights, alone,*
> *The flesh defiled by dreams of flesh,*
> *Rehearsed desire dead in spring,*
> *How shall we return?*[25]

Ezekiel's anxiety is understandable. He adjudges that the whole humanity, instead of remaining centralized in itself, marches into innumerable inauthentic directions prompted by selfishness and desires, 'the flesh defiled by dreams of flesh'[26] He condemns humanity as 'debtors to the whore of Love/Corrupted by the things imagined'[27] The idea of humanity diverting itself from the centre is reminiscent of *The Second Coming* of W.B. Yeats:

Turning and turning in the widening gyre
The falcon cannot hear the falconer.[28]

Out of ourselves love prompted by the dreams of flesh we have forgotten the invaluable message of Jesus, which he propagated through charity and self-sacrifice. These biblical over-tones are implied and suggestive. The expression 'We who leave the house in April, Lord', might as well have been prompted by T.S. Eliot's *The Wasteland,* which starts with a negative celebration of April, says T.S. Eliot:

April is the cruelest month, breeding
Lilacs out of the dead land, mixing
Memory and desire, stirring
Dull roots with spring rain.[29]

Incidentally *A Time to Change* is the title poem in Ezekiel's first poetical publication. The implicit reference to W.B. Yeats and T.S. Eliot is Ezekiel's manner of paying tributes and obeisance to these great masters. At the same time, it is noteworthy here that Geoffery Chaucer, the father of English literature, also starts his *The Canterbury Tales* by way of celebrating April:

Whan that Aprille with his shoures soote. . .[30]

Ezekiel appears to suggest that, if we centralize ourselves in ourselves, there is certainly a way out from all the corruptions of life. Home, in the sense of one's own self, is in fact the place where we belong. In the home there is 'the juice of life.' It is for us to make a right choice, says Ezekiel:

The juice of life is in us still
But when the mind determines everything
The leap is never made, the music
Never quite completed, redemption
Never fully won.[31]

Ironically speaking 'return' back to the house is only possible when we drift from the house. This is a sort of drifting off 'the house' (i.e., the self).

The Leap of Faith

Ezekiel's suggestion is very common. But, however, if only we can return we can be completely redeemed. Since our mind determines everything, and our mind being the flirting agent the most required 'leap is never made'. This leap is leap of 'faith'. Practically speaking scriptures always spoke about this leap of faith. Nissim Ezekiel appears to state that in our human set this 'leap of faith' is not possible. What all he ultimately prompts here is a just realization that there are 'secret faults are concealed in us'. These secret faults have to be accepted, and a trial has always to be made to clarify them for ourselves. When we look to the mystery of God's creation and understand his design of creation the whole world becomes an enchanting one. It is in this God's manner of creation that we too have to endorse our creative activity. This we can do by way of living in the here and now, without imaginatively turning ourselves either to the past or to the future. This is all what Ezekiel means by centralizing ourselves in the 'house'. What all he suggests is we have to live our lives in the 'here and now' and perform our creative works in the same manner. Ezekiel endorses for himself a poetical commitment to create his poems as spontaneous and immediate reflections of living in the 'here and now'.

The Metaphysical Strain

Ever since T.S. Eliot and others fondly revived a new taste for the British metaphysical poets, there emerged into modern poetry a rare impressionistic phenomena of placing contradictory and antithetical images. This poetic process of assembling the contradictory and antithetical images and ideas was categorically described by Dr. Johnson as 'the most heterogeneous ideas are yolked by violence together'.[32]

For the eighteeth-century critics the metaphysical poetry of John Donne appeared as something to be set aside. The very expression metaphysical is derogatory. The eighteenth century is a new classical era, and their thrust for sublime aesthetic demands is understandable. But with the change of the senerio from the eighteenth to the twentieth through the nineteenth century, totally revised the aesthetic sensibilities also, *inter-elia,* our very attitudes and dispositions to the world of existence. The age-old scholasticism in literature gave way to what the moderns call 'the expression of experience'.

If poetry and all other arts are a matter of expressing the experience by way of adopting a manner of 'saying', the scholastic pursuits of sublimity are totally set aside. In its place the 'formulaes of exquisteness on ecstasy', through the colloquial speech rhythms, came into force. The modern symbolists and imagists guided the modern poetic sensibility, Loconic Juxtapositions and emotional gaps in the speech rhythms became fashionable. In short poetry shifted to the spoken manner of writing. The ancient metaphysical poets, though Browning, paved the way for the modern poetry.

However, the twentieth-century poets distinctly distinguished ecstasy itself as a matter of infelt feeling of novelty in comprehending the world of experience. It so every experience supported by emotions, feelings, imaginations, and ideas is likely to imprint its marks of novelty on the experiencing self.

The Modernness of the Modern Poetry

For the moderns it is this experiencing self, with the help of imagination, that becomes poetical. In their approach for the poetic introspective modalities of expression, the moderns prefer to place heterogeneous and antithetical ideas, feelings and emotions side by side. What the great Dr. Johnson called the 'process of heterogeneous ideas being yolkds together by violence' categorically alters itself as a process of Loconic Juxtaposition. Ezra Pound substantially demonstrated the abundant aesthetic worth of this Loconic Juxtaposition. The finest example is to be found in his 'In a Station of the Metro':

The apparition of these faces in the crowd;
Petals on a wet, black bough.[33]

These two lines of Ezra Pound are an eternal puzzle. They 'tease us out of thought', as does the *Grecian Urn*[34] of John Keats. The following lines of Ezekiel are exactly as riddle-like as the above lines of Ezra Pound:

A death mask
A phoenix egg.

And sundry decorations,
not without meaning.[35]

The poetic formula of Loconic Juxtapositions recieved its highest aesthetic credentials in the hands of Baudelaire's *'Aesthetique D'Mal (The Aesthetic of Evils)'* and T.S. Eliot's *The Waste-Land.* In addition to T.S. Eliot and Baudelaire and many other great poets of the twentieth century like W.B. Yeats, W.H. Auden, Louis MacNeice, Stephen Spender, Ted Hughes and scores of others tried this Loconic Juxtapositional technique successfully.

It may not be out of place to state here that of all the Indo-Anglian poets, it is Nissim Ezekiel that implemented this poetic technique of Loconic Juxtapositions in a very successful manner. In this process, he closely follow foot steps of T.S. Eliot. Very often it appears that he substantially created poetic analogies to the poems of T.S. Eliot.

Ezekiel celebrates the city in all its discarded dimensions; and talks of modern civilization itself in the very depressive tones of loss and anxiety. In all his poetry the pursuit of his personal identity is fundamental. On arriving at the stand that the loss of identity is a certain dehumanizing factor in our times, Ezekiel turns out to be a concerned poet searching for identity. He expresses his anxiety at the loss of identity in innumerable ways. In order to express his anxiety at modern man's meaningless manner of existence. He has to say as follows in his *The Stone*:

I have learnt to love the texture of a stone
Rough or smooth but all unyielding stone,
Which plays no facile game of outward show
And holds itself together as a bone;

It does not feel the paralysing flow
Of everything that is not hard as stone
But shares its nature like the hidden bone.[36]

The juxtaposition of 'the texture of his tone with the hidden bone' is not a mere matter of the use of pun. It goes far beyond. The poem compels on a comparison with the following passage in T.S. Eliot's *The Waste-land*. In the context of T.S. Eliot we have that fearful invitation when he said:

(Come in under the shadow of this red rock),
And I will show you something different from either
Your shadow at morning striding behind you
Or your shadow at evening rising to meet you:
I will show you fear in handful of dust.[37]

The all unyielding stone of Ezekiel is symbolically expressive of the external world of experience, which permanently alludes comprehension. But, however, this objective world is not a 'facile game of outward show'. In being an understandable mystery it puts a perennial challenge to the inner authenticity of his person. Thereby, the all-embracing mysterious universe 'holds itself together as a bone'. The bone refers to the inner vitality which makes man equally and courageously in opposition to the world existence.

Just like the inner skeletal frame makes man capable of standing errect as one like himself and none like the other, Ezekiel wants to suggests that the necessary 'courage-to-be' comes to man with the help of these inner convictions (the hidden bones). He wants to understand the stony world, which behaves itself in the manner of Heraclatian flux and not in the Demacraitus atomic jumble. The Demacraitus definition that 'atom is the smallest particle of matter' does not hold good. The inner courage of man (i.e., the bone) may not be powerful enough to 'feel the parallelizing flow' of everything that is not hard as stone. It, however, 'shares its (the stone's) nature', by way of standing in opposition 'like the hidden bone' (inner courage). As S.N. Prasad rightly pointed out:

> *His concern is not with his single self alone,*
> *But with the selves of others also because he*
> *has a genuine concern for the welfare of his*
> *people, Indian people.*[38]

With all his Christ-like charity in his mind he says in his poem *Blessings* that :

> *Be drunk, occasionally,*
> *but not with gin*
> *or whisky. May the Lord*
> *use you up for ends*
> *beyond your means,*
> *so you know what drunkenness*
> *really means.*[39]

'This drunkenness' in the real sense concerns with over-powering oneself with spiritual performances. The prayer that do Lord may use you up for ends/beyond your mean's suggests at what Jesus himself had done in the last supper, when he offered bread and wine to his disciples. This bread and wine piously suggests the flesh and blood of Jesus Christ according to the Catholic Christian formula of on substations. In the Protestant cults the ritual is reterminated as trans-substation. In both the cases, there is stern expectancy of extreme devotion towards Lords, The Maker in Ezekiel's poems need not be interpreted as Christian formulas. The Christ-like charity and devotion formula is ultimately a great humanistic formula of spiritual self-contentment. That way Ezekiel is not a religious bigot, in spite of his *Hymns in Darkness.* Whereas he is referring to the Christian ritualistic complexities of above poem, more or less in the same categorical manner he refers to the Hindu axiomatic myth of reincarnation or rebirth in his 'Night of the Scorpion'. There in Ezekiel says:

> *May the sins of your previous birth*
> *be burned away tonight they said.*
> *May your suffering decrease*
> *the misfortunes of your next birth, they said.*[40]

In this context Ezekiel is sarcastic and ironic in his tone, whereas in the biblical analogy of the previous quotation he is sublimely serious.

His Ironic Vision of Poetic Process

All this goes to suggest that Ezekiel adopted for himself a stern cosmic vision of the world and tracks it through his poetic techniques of metaphysical Loconic Juxtapositions. The best poem that summarizes his metaphysical poetic practice is to be found in his *Poet, Lover and Birdwatcher.* The *Poet, Lover and Birdwatcher* is a compact poetic experiment, which shows the mastery of the poet in handling the English meters. It is written in two stanzas of ten lines each. But, however, the intentional dimensions of the poet in parallelizing the 'Poet' with 'Lover' and 'Birdwatcher' are obviously light-hearted, even extending to mock-heroic proportions. The comparison itself, instead of giving any sublime elevation in the readers mind it proposes a mere casual light-heartedness in so far as the metaphysical manner of associating the inner phenomenal modalities of the *Poet, Lover and Birdwatcher.*

That the intentions of Ezekiel are quite non-serious is obvious from the title of the poem itself, which is a typical dialectic manner of turning against himself. Elsewhere in his *Background Casually* also Ezekiel initiates the poem with the following lines: 'A poet-rascal-clown was born.'[41] 'The clownish and cartoonist technique of proposing the title in triplex that go to turn against the poet is quite humorous, and delicately reflective of the casual manner of the poet, with help of which he takes his readers into a charming confidence.

What all Ezekiel wants to suggest in the 'Poet, Lover and Birdwatcher' concerns with the inner phenomenal processes of the activities in the unconscious selves of the three. In the pseudo romantic manner he considers that the processes of emergence into results is mysterious and undeniable. In the meantime before the results emerge all the three are required to wait patiently. This is to say that they are not required to do anything at all, except sitting like clowns or idiots. The parallelism between the three is interesting, poetically speaking the parallelism itself in its uncanny manner suggests the jest.

There is no way of reading any serious or sublime intentions on the part of the poet in clubbing the three unclubbable representatives as agents. 'Ezekiel quite naughtily suggests that all the three are categorically fated to something that would happen quite accidental. In their incapacitated manner of their waiting for the final outcome categorically relates to the state of patients. The agent patient phenomenal manner of being in the world, which is prominently suggested by the great writers like William Shakespeare and T.S. Eliot, has been light-heartedly proposed here. All the three are expected to wait on unendingly until the final effects follow.

The critics like B.K. Das, S.C. Sengupta and A.V. Sahane arduously contended that Ezekiel's poem *Poet, Lover and Birdwatcher* is a sublime classical peace of work of art. B.K. Das goes to the extent of calling it' . . . the greatest landmark in Ezekiel's poetry'. It epitomizes Ezekiel's search for poetry, while the 'greatest landmark' certificate is quite dubious (there are many other great poems of Ezekiel). 'The seach for poetics' is quite undependable, in the sense that Ezekiel as a poet closely followed by modern European poets, by way of creating typical analogies for the great twentieth-century masterpieces. Again B.K. Das's contention, that the poets do not compose the poem but the poems are found is an obvious statement of extended pathetic fallacy. Ezekiel himself is a great ironist and satirist. The very ideas of inventing a parallelism between 'Poet, Lover and Birdwatcher' is funny and humorous.

S.C. Sengupta went a step ahead of B.K. Das when he stated that Ted Hughes *Thought Fox* and Ezekiel's *Poet, Lover and Birdwatcher* are 'exercises in poetic process'. While Ted Hughes is pertinently talking about the emergence of thought as a sudden phenomenal occurrence from out of the simmering darkness of imagination like a fox, it has nothing to do with poetry as a process. Thought is certainly a very important component in poetry but not a substitute for poetry at all. So the comparison between two poems is unattainable.

That Ezekiel has written this poem in a mock ironic

manner is reduceable from the last line: 'The deaf can hear, the blind can recover sight'.[42]

Precisely speaking Nissim Ezekiel is not a bluebladed romantic, who considers poetry as a matter of divine inspirations. The poem *Poet, Lover and Birdwatcher* is an ironic assertion on the old romantic poetics. Speaking of the poetic process as a creative activity, B.K. Das in his *The Pattern of "Thought in Poet, Lover, Birdwatcher,"* says as follow:

> *This poem – the crowning dome to the edifice that is 'The Exact Name' – is, in a sense the dome of Nissim Ezekiel's entire poetry. It is impossible to overemphasize the momentous significance of this poem. It stands as the greatest landmark in Ezekiel's poetry. It epitomizes Nissim Ezekiel's search for poetic.*[43]

Continuity of Life and Personal Importance

Nissim Ezekiel continues his poetic practice with the prime purpose of making a balance between poetry and life. As a matter of fact how his poetry is impressionistic expression of the instant poetical moments of his own personal life. Therefore, the tone of his poetry is autobiographical. His poems are not to be misconceived as autobiographical glorification. Living in our times is rather a crisis filled with painful experience. This crisis in life and its pain are matter of everybody's experience. His attitude to life is coupled with passion for enjoyment. His sensitive and sensible emotions are capable of putting certain insight into the life around him. But his reflections are always personal. His inherent poetic curiosity forces his to make certain statements which are likely to fulfil themselves as poetic aphorisms.

It was Ezra Pound who once said that if a poet could create even one permanently lasting image out of his life work, his poetical credentials are laudable. Nissim Ezekiel arrives at such important poetical images and ideas, with the rare felicity of a critic, abounding in poetic visions. Effecting a balance and harmony between life and poetry and the pure biological fact of existence is the work of a poet. The words of Michael Garman are worth repeating here. Says Garman:

> *He is a poet of whom it is not trivial to say that his poetry and his life are inextricable, and whose purpose in writing is to make a harmony (life, poetry) out of a purely biological fact (existence).*[44]

The inextricable nature of his poetry and life is progressively available right from the beginning. In *The Poster Poem* and *The Poster Prayers* (1973) the personal nature of his poetry becomes substantially available. His voice becomes very much conspicuous in being a personal search for convictions and determinations. At this level it all becomes again to borrow the expression of M. Garman: '. . . a synthetic comprehension of traditions or themes, or even a reconciliation of opposites'.[45] It is in this process of synthesizing the opposites that Ezekiel falls upon his most favourite theme of dream and reality. His dreams are human and simple. Says Ezekiel:

> *The singing voice*
> *To utter praise*
> *A bit of land*
> *A woman too*
> *Grapes or figs*

And metaphors
Insight illumination
Secret faults concealed no more.[46]

This forms the concluding part of the title poem *A Time to Change* of his first collection. Being a poet of Bombay his personal dreamy aspirations for pastrol simplicities of life are understandable. Even 'fig' would do if 'grapes' are not easily available. But a woman, a singing voice and metaphors are sufficient for him to fulfil his demands of life, as such. But when it comes to the utmost maturity as a poet his poetic demands become the most substantial cries of the occasion. Here the synthesis of reality and dream is potentially metaphorized into a serious self-search. A mere complacent metaphor or the ordinary provisions of life would not do. Says Ezekiel:

To make them right
you so what had
to be done in any case.[47]

His poetical convictions are clear. He has to completely extricate himself from the social, cultural, ethical and moral traditional and formal features of life. Like a raging rebellion he says:

There's no other way
except to burn
your bridges, bury your dead.[48]

If so, he is not pining for a synthesis. On the other hand, he is searching for courage to substantiate his human convictions as a rebellious poet.

Therefore, he says:

And not in
alcoholic language
but in some needed flame.[49]

And again Ezekiel says:

I do not want the ashes
of the old fire but the flame itself.[50]

The expression 'alcoholic language' stands for passive complacent, and self-deluding metaphors of his poetic start, the language that sends you to sleep and dream. This would not do. Life is excruciatingly intricate. This is both internal and external. Therefore, he commits himself for 'some needful flame'. The requisite needful flame can be supplied by a rare and unique passion to know. Knowing from an introspective angle is always an act of knowing oneself. This is possible when you burn the bridges of the past and bury them. Even with this kind of rage it is not really possible for the poet to be able to awake himself. The complete awakened state or a real total extrication from the past would not be available for him. He has an ardent desire to live in the here and now. But life itself in its macro-spectrum is a continuance; and man has to slavishly depend upon time itself, as a helpless patient. But, however, the most cherished desires of the poet for a 'needed flame' gets recorded here in an inspired and emotional manner. But, the sleep itself is a reality and all the dreams are near half-awakenings. Therefore, his demand for the 'needed flame' would never be satisfied, and a synthesis or balance between dream and reality would not be possible. That agony was potentially expressed by the poets like Baudelaire, T.S. Eliot, W.H. Auden and W.B. Yeats. Their agony is universal and it engulfs the entire humanity in the name of urbanization and civilization. Therefore, in the title of the poem 'The Poet Contemplates His Inaction'; is quite expressive of the extraordinary painful impoverished nature of the poet himself. Says Ezekiel:

> *Half awakened*
> *he looks again at his*
> *wrong, time, wrong place:*[51]

This is a blind statement. Retracing the idea that man never grows in wisdom he arrives at the stand of finding himself in a 'wrong time, wrong place'. Therefore, his awareness is always a half truth envisaging the point that man in his pursuit of knowledge nearly shifts from one ignorance to the other; and most complacently, he thinks that he is acquiring the new knowledge. This is the real fallacy. Therefore, he always finds himself in a 'wrong time, wrong place'. Michael Garman's statement that:

> *. . . .his poetry and his life are inextricable, and whose purpose in writing is to make harmony (life, poetry) out of a purely biological fact (existence).*[52]

is at the best a mere half truth in the context of Ezekiel. Therefore, he bents upon acquiring a poetic insight with 'secret faults concealed no more'. If so he wants to make a whole-hearted confession of his poetic unrest through self-search and self-criticism.

The real urgency of Ezekiel's poetry lies in its evocatively critical manner of denouncing what all he finds in the name of life within him as well as around him. Therefore, he is a bitter critic of humanity on behalf of the new humanism. The critical stands of Ezekiel are invariably informed by his mature human judgement. But, however, he does not adopt for himself the stance of a total nihilist. He is of a conviction that life, with all its insufficiencies and shortcomings has to be lived on 'as is where is basis'. The poetic involvement in this context is only a matter of expressing these experiences of living the life-in-itself, and life-for-itself. It cannot be said that he hates life as such. But, he denounces the life styles which are inauthentic and insufficient. Ezekiel all through his poetry gently exposed the inauthentic and insufficient manner in which people live their lives, without ever coming to grasp the immense humanity, which is their only refuge of life in the world of existence.

People, unfortunately live their lives in the mechanical dog-holes prepared by the cultures, the traditions, and the age-old positive philosophies of life, which go to make their institutions the most rigid entities. According to Ezekiel life has to be lived by way of asserting ones own freedom and choice at every moment of existence. Any amount of degradations or dwindlings from this canon of life makes life an insufferable crisis. Says Ezekiel:

United by our ignorance
we struggle, and the words
materialise, begin to matter.
Is this surprising, unusual?
Not at all. Language
is our conspicuous gift: The Word,

made flesh, is sought again.
We make it as we make our lives.[53]

If so, the real liberator of humanity is language as poetry.

Poetic Sense and Sensibility

Ezekiel categorically states in his *Poet, Lover and Birdwatcher* that the 'best poet waits for words.'[54] An ornichologist's sit by the hill side in silence by the flowing river, and a lover waits for his beloved till she 'no longer waits but risks surrendering—'[55]. The parallelisms are very nice observation as properties of certain acts. The Birdwatcher's end is in spotting a new species of birds. A lovers destination is in seeking the abrupt surrender of his beloved. The poet's achievement is measured by the worth of the poem he writes. This is to say that composing a poem is an episodic achievement. In this context, there is a major differences between poem and poetry for Ezekiel. In his poem *Poetry* he brings out this distinction very clearly. Says Ezekiel:

A poem is an episode completed
In an hour or two, but poetry
Is something more. It is the why
The how the what, the flow
From which a poem comes...[56]

The last line of this poem are much more important than the above:

. . . the residue
Is what you read, as a poem, the rest
Flows and is poetry. This should be so,
Precisely so.[57]

Therefore, it is 'poetry' and not any poem that is important for a poet. In the 'Poet, Lover and Birdwatcher' he speaks of the dawn of poetic sense:

> *. . . and sense is found*
> *By poets lost in crooked, restless flight.*[58]

As has already been suggested poetry for Ezekiel is a matter of personal experience; and worth of personal experience a matter of right correspondence established between is sense and sensibility of being in the world. There is always a spirited struggle on the part of Ezekiel to save himself from the 'dissociation of sensibility',[59] syndrome of T.S. Eliot. To that extent he is honest to the core. And makes his sense clear by way of turning against himself in the following lines. Says Ezekiel:

> *The Eternal Ego speaks*
> *Suppose I were a shooting-star,*
> *I would want to be seen.*
> *That would be my only meaning.*
> *What is there, after all,*
> *in shooting across the sky*
> *and being burnt up ?*
> *But being seen!*
> *That would be another thing.*[60]

His earnest desire is to be 'seen' in the true perspective of his being as a poet. It was Wallace Stevens who said that 'a poem is a poem not because it is a poem, but because of personal sensibility'. Ezekiel appears to reconcile himself to this idea whole-heartedly. Again in what Ezekiel says 'the residue is what you read, as a poem', he totally borrows the idea of Wallace Stevens in what he said 'a poet comes to poetry just as a tree comes to twigs'. The fact is the real poetic sensibility is an ever continuing and never resting phenomena, just like life itself. Therefore, the 'rest flows and is poetry'. Ezekiel's *After Reading a Prediction,* he very bluntly declared that it:

> *. . . was always my ambition;*
> *and to rage against the barren*
> *not only in friend or stranger*
> *but perfectly familiar*
> *in my own signature.*[61]

The expression the 'rage against the barren' is very important. 'Barren' in the sense of infertile to the widest spread unfeeling quality amongst people in our times. It is this unfeeling quality, through lack of correspondence between sense and sensibility. There emerges the rampant vulgarity in the heart of the world. Most ironically Ezekiel chastises the colossal lack of sincerity towards personal experience in his *Transparently.* In it Ezekiel explains what is fallenness in man. He says:

> *. . .I still rush off*
> *in every direction at once*
> *and fall for every bait.*[62]

Right from the European Renaissance a race for achievement emerged as a fundamental manner of existence in the minds of the people. In this race for achievement the people always bothered about destination, goals, by way of driving themselves greater achievements than anybody else. In this mad race for achievements man's sense of living up to the moral niceties of life, which constitutes the humanness in man, was shamelessly overlooked. Again, by way of turning against himself ironically Ezekiel states in the above poem:

Who wants experience
at the cost of achievement?
All I want now
is the recognition
of dilemma
and the quickest means
of resolving it
within my limits.[63]

Immediately preceding these lines he makes it very clear what he calls the 'dilemma', and the urgency of resolving it with 'the quickest means of resolving is what all he detests in his fellow man'. Life has to be lived in its fullness and ease. The wnole generation has fallen off from this important formula of existence. Therefore, he states

It is a falling. . .
a most terrible thing.
And what one learns
is not all that important
because one has learnt it already,
over and over again.[64]

The presumptuous and complicant manner in which people take it for granted that they had 'learnt it already over and over again' is highly deplorable. It speaks of the careless urgency in which man lives. We should not forget that Ezekiel is an existential thinker. Therefore, the dilemma of existence permanently remains as an 'either/or' the dilemma of Keirkegaard. There is no way of solving this dilemma with the help of any 'quickest means'. With this kind of temperament Ezekiel made for himself the following determination in his *Background Casually,* he states:

> *I have made my commitments now.*
> *This is one; to stay where I am,*
> *As others choose to give themselves*
> *In some remote and backward place.*
> *My backwards place is where I am.*[65]

With this kind of determination he proceeds on his poetic journey, a journey which is in itself and for itself. Like Robert Frost he does not have 'miles to go before I sleep'.[66] His journey is not worldly. The same thought he states in his *Morning Prayer*:

> *God grant me certainty*
> *In kinships with the sky,*
> *Air, earth, fire, sea*
> *And the fresh inward eye.*[67]

What he says at the end of *Morning Prayer* is all important. He prays:

> *God grant me the metaphor*
> *To make it human good.*[68]

But, however Ezekiel is absolutely conscious of the illusive worth of metaphors. The real metaphor which has to stand as an equivalent correspondence to life itself is never achieved successfully. Hence a poet, while being a poet, is never complete. A great insufficiency always remains in spite of all this sincere efforts. This is so because of the simple fact that the personal experience as a property never repeats itself. No apt comparison or contrast is possible. At the same time experience is a never ending and ever continuing phenomena of inner process. Addressing God in his *Theological* he has to say as follows:

I've stripped off a hundred veils
and still there are more
that cover your Creation.
Why are you so elusive?[69]

He concludes the poem with the following lines:

You seem to say
that it's all up to me.
What a terrible situation
Your Divine Love has created.
Or has Something Other
Created it
and you are
only trying
to save it?
Anyway, at the moment,
I am very tired of it.[70]

The very doubt he shows in stating whether his is *Divine Love* or something other force that created this world, speaks of his metaphysical rebellious temper. The everyday world of life, which functions itself as an insoluable riddle, creates in him a great sense of exhaust and tired someness. This is what he called

a deep affection for the world
With words emerging from a contrite heart.[71]

Out of this 'deep affection' he grooms the world of nature, of fellowmen, and of himself In this affectionate poetic journey, if he:

> *Finds, on a lucky lay, a metaphor*
> *Leaping from the sod.*
> *If this is not a miracle*
> *Then I am God.*[72]

God's world is a miracle; and to the extend that the human personality is a part of this God's world, it is also equally a miracle. It is this miraculous nature of his personal sensibility that always aims at poetically establishing a right correspondence with the sense of being in the world. The outcome is his expressionistic, poetry that evaluates the objective world in his inner consciousness. That world of experience he creates is bound to be novel and interesting. Inspite of all this exact correspondence between the subjective and the objective world of things are not possible. This aspect of Nissim Ezekiel's poetry will be taken up in the following Chapter.

REFERENCES

1. Robert Con Davis and Ronald Scheifer, *Contemporary Literary Criticism: Literary and Cultural Studies* (New York: Longman, 1989), p. 15.
2. K.R.S. Lyengar, *Indian Writing in English* (New Delhi: Sterling Publishers Pvt. Ltd., 1989) p. 641.
3. *Ibid.*, p. 657.
4. *Ibid.*, p. 660.
5. *Ibid.*,
6. Nissim Ezekiel, 'What is Indian in Indo-English Poetry', *Osmania Journal of English Studies*, Vol. XIX, (1983), p. 49.
7. D.J. Enright and E.D. Chickera, *English Critical Texts: 16th*

Century to 20th Century (London: Oxford University Press, 1962), p. 308.

8. Inder Nath Kher, *Journal of South Asian Literature*, Vol. XI, Nos. 3-4 (Spring, Summer 1976), p. 12.
9. Nissim Ezekiel, *A Time to Change* (London: Fortune Press, 1952), no pagination.
10. *Ibid.*
11. Inder Nath Kher, ed., *Journal of South Asian Uterature*, Vol. XI, Nos 3-4, (Spring, Summer 1976), p. 4.
12. Nissim Ezekiel, *A Time to Change* (London: Fortune Press, 1952).
13. *Ibid.*
14. Nissim Ezekiel, *The Third* (Bombay: Strand Bookshop, 1959), no pagination.
15. Inder Nath Kher, ed., *Journal* of *South Asian Literature*, Vol XI, Nos. 3-4 (Spring, Summer 1976), p. 557.
16. Nissim Ezekiel, *A Time to Change* (London: Fortune Press, 1952), no pagination.
17. *Ibid.*
18. Inder Nath Kher, ed., *Journal of Sourth Asian Literature*, Vol. XI, Nos 3-4 (Spring, Summer 1976), p. 87.
19. *Ibid.*,
20. *Ibid.*,
21. *Ibid.*, p. 88.
22. *Ibid.*, p. 257.
23. Inder Nath Kher, ed., *Journal* of *Sourth Asian Literature*, Vol. XI, Nos. 3-4 (Spring, Summer 1976), p. 256.
24. *Ibid.*, p. 254.
25. Nissim Ezekiel, *A Time to Change* (London: Fortune Press, 1952).
26. *Ibid.*
27. *Ibid.*
28. Michael Roberts, ed., *The Fabers Books of Modern Verse* (London: Faber and Faber Ltd., 1965), p. 58.
29. *Ibid.*, p. 91.
30. E.L.B.S., ed., *Fifteen Poets* (Calcutta: Oxford University Press, Faraday House, 1941), p. 8.

31. Inder Nath Kher, ed., *Journal of Sourth Asian Literature,* Vol. XI, Nos. 3-4 (Spring, Summer 1976), p. 11.
32. D.J. Enright and E.D. Chickera, *English Critical Text, 16th Century to 20th Century* (London: Oxford University Press, 1962), p. 304.
33. Nina Baymed, *The Norton Anthology of American Literature,* (New York : W.W. Norton & Co., 1986), p. 1774.
34. E.L.B.S., ed., *Fifteen Poets,* (Calcutta: Oxford University Press, Faraday House, 1941), p. 358.
35. Inder Nath Kher, ed., *Journal* of *South Asian Literature,* Vol. XI, Nos. 3-4 (Spring, Summer 1976), p. 125.
36. *Ibid.,* p. 25.
37. Michael Roberts, ed., *The Fabers Books of Modern Verse* (London: Faber and Faber Ltd., 1965), p. 125.
38. S.N. Prasad, "The Cognitive Self in Nissim Ezekiel: An Approach to his Poetry", *Indian English Uterature: Since Independence,* ed. Paniker K. Ayyappa (New Delhi: The Indian Association for English Studies, 1991), p. 133.
39. *Ibid.,* p. 132.
40. Inder Nath Kher, ed., *Journal* of *South Asian Uterature,* Vol. XI, Nos. 3-4 (Spring, Summer 1976), p. 72.
41. *Ibid.,* p. 85.
42. *Ibid.,* p. 75.
43. G.S. Balaram Gupta, ed. *The Journal of Indian Writings in English,* Vol. VII (July 1979), p. 46.
44. Inder Nath Kher, ed., *Journal of South Asian Literature,* Vol. XI, Nos. 3-4, (Spring, Summer 1976), p. 209.
45. *Ibid.*
46. Nissim Ezekiel, *A Time of Change* (London: Fortune Press 1952).
47. Inder Nath Kher, ed., *Journal of South Asian Literature,* Vol. XI, Nos. 3-4 (Spring, Summer 1976), p. 152.
48. *Ibid.,*
49. *Ibid.,*
50. *Ibid.,* p. 147.
51. *Ibid.,* p. 152.
52. *Ibid.,* p. 209.

53. *Ibid.*, p. 148.
54. Nissim Ezekiel, *Latter-Day Psalms* (Delhi: Oxford University Press, 1982), p. 52.
55. *Ibid.*, p. 53.
56. Inder Nath Kher, ed., *Journal of South Asian Literature*, Vol. XI, Nos. 3-4 (Spring, Summer 1976), p. 17.
57. *Ibid.*,
58. Saleem Peeradina, ed., *Contemporary Indian Poetry in English* (Delhi: Macmillan, 1972), p. 12.
59. D.J. Enright and E.D. Chickera, *English Critical Text: 16th Century to 20th Century* (London: Oxford University Press, 1962), p. 308.
60. Inder Nath Kher, ed., *Journal of South Asian Literature*, Vol. XI, Nos. 3-4 (Spring, Summer 1976), p. 131.
61. *Ibid.*, p. 97.
62. *Ibid.*, p. 87.
63. *Ibid.*, p. 88.
64. *Ibid.*,
65. Saleem Peeradina, ed., *Contemporary Indian Poetry in English An Assessment and Selection* (Delhi: Macmillan, 1972), p. 7.
66. Egbert S. Oliver, ed., *American Literature: 1890-1965 An Anthology* (New Delhi: Eurasia Publishing House, 1994), p. 406.
67. Nissim Ezekiel, *Latter-Day Psalms* (Delhi: Oxford University Press, 1982), p. 61.
68. *Ibid.*,
69. Inder Nath Kher, ed., *Journal of South Asian Literature*, Vol. XI, Nos. 3-4 (Spring, Summer 1976), p. 99.
70. *Ibid.*,
71. M.K. Naik, S.K. Desai and G.S. Amur, eds., *Critical Essays on Indian Writing in English* (Dharwar : Karnatak University, 1968).
72. Inder Nath Kher, ed., *Journal* of *South Asian Literature*, Vol. XI, Nos. 3-4 (Spring, Summer 1976), p. 211.

3

The Divided Soul

Nissim Ezekiel as a poet, in spite of his unified purpose of representing modernity, often gets divided between his personal choices and poetic commitments. A poet, who started as a skeptic in his *A Time to Change* gradually metamorphosies himself into a religious poet by the time he comes to his *Hymns in Darkness.*

To a large extent, Ezekiel is a romantic idealist nurturing in himself innumerable dreams for a free and felicitous India. But, however, it is worth noting that romanticism as a poetic movement died its natural death after W.B. Yeats and a few other British poets. Therefore, Ezekiel, when he particularly stressed on the old romantic ideals, looks slightly outlandish and even decadent, not condescending, however, to the decadent poetic culture of the Georgian poets. At the same time, he inherits the immediate Western naturalize—realist traditions through education and culture. As a result, he develops a tone of defiance and non-confornism extending to skeptical dimensions. Hopelessness, deprivity and loss of faith are there everywhere for him to see; but, however, through his poetic endeavour he always wanted to arrive at 'a bold nectarean answer for the poison of the present'[1]. His great search for nectarean answer always hastened him towards maintaining hopeful deductions form out of what he experienced as hopeless performer in operation. It is here that his authentic self falls at its 'either/or' dilemma: and thereby, the division of his soul is there to see for everybody: The exact division in his mind does not concern itself with any philosophical concept are with his disagreements with the world of existence on principles his passion for the traditional poetic techniques and his inner urge for introspection make him categorically divided in his commitments. At the outset he wants to truly and realistically represent the decadent Indian social scenario in his poems. At the same time, he nurtured in himself very lofty humanistic ideals, which come to the forefront in English poetry as, introspective moments of meditations. His passion for realism as a craftsman and his urge of maintaining himself a high humanistic idealism divides him into distinctly two different poets, in fact, Ezekiel's observational moments and his introspective meditative moments bring forth two distinct kinds of poetry. One is ironic and satirical; the ether is a passionate formula of creating apt metaphors for his inner spiritual experiences. His *Hymns in Darkness* is full of such spiritual alienation. *A Time to Change* and *The Unfinished Man* contain innumerable ironic and satirical pictures of life. In this context the words of P. Lal are worth quoting:

> *Mr. Nissim Ezekiel is, I think, one of our better poets because he is the most consistent in maintaining a happy balance between experiment in technique and the Introspective urge.*[2]

In this context the words of M. David are also worth quoting:

> *Nissim Ezekiel who is surely one of the most accomplished of Indian poet writing in English today: his disciplined spareness and panstaking choice of words serve an acute and ironic sensibility continually harrowed by the discrepancy between public face and private feeling:*
>
> *Beneath his daily strategy,*
> *Reflected in his suffering face,*
> *I see his dim identity –*
> *A small, deserted, holy place.*[3]

But, however, one thing that consolidates his poetic stand is to be found in the unifiedness of his personal experiences which ultimately go to take his analogical poetic forms. The apparent dilemma gets resolved in the uniqueness of his personal experiences. His poetry, to borrow the expression of W. Stevens: 'is a medium of personal experience'. The uniqueness of this 'personal' temper or temperament of Ezekiel's poetry gets established in this Chapter.

The Romantic Idealism vs the Modern Temper

While his aesthetic concerns are formerly nurtured by the British Romantics, including W. Blake, his modernist temper or temperament gets nurtured by the new humanism, that came to the portion after 1890s in Europe. Most of the poems of Ezekiel in the beginning of his career are prompted by romantic aspirations. In his poem 'Poetry' Ezekiel states as follows:

A poem is an episode, completed
In an hour or two, but poetry
Is something more. It is the why
The how the what, the flow
From which a poem comes,[4]

All the romantic poets their formal poems are mere occasional of their permanent and continual poetic personality. For William Wordsworth:

> *... poetry is the spontaneous overflow of powerful feelings: it takes its origin from emotion recollected in tranquillity:*[5]

Having taken such an origin, an ideal poem for Wordsworth grows into an instinctive and instantaneous formula of combining the choices, emotions and feelings. It ultimately converges into an aesthetic submission through a sort of muscial ensemble. The story of the poetic process of almost all the romantics is more or less the same. In the case of P.B. Shelley it gets formed from the divine and mysterious sources; and for John Keats it takes it thrill from the perennial mystery of the felt feelings and emotions nurtured by his mysterious sense properties.

The Mystery of Poetry

In all probability poetry is a mystery for the romantics. For Ezekiel too these mysterious properties of poetry are true. But, however, his progressive idealism of poetry, so far it its structural contingencies are concerned it takes its shape from the humanistic and the historical dimensions of the human mind. As all other modern poets he is highly individualistic and sceptical. He prefers to stand in opposition to what all that is suggested by nature by fellowman, and even by himself. Therefore, a permanent ring of doubt, interrogation and suspicion on revertebrates although his poetry. In stating that a poem 'is the why/ the how, the what, the flow/from which a poem comes', his interrogative temper is ultimately is what he emulated from the twentieth-century poet of Europe like Ezra Pound, W.B. Yeats, T.S. Eliot, and all other masters. Loconic Juxtapositions technique of the symbols, images and all such expressionistic devices of poetry are directly borrowed from T.S. Eliot. The overall frustrated spirit of Ezekiel comes from W.B. Yeats and all his mythic propoundations.

The division of the two sublime forces in him is not contradictory. Both the temperamental properties of Ezekiel seek a poetic confluence, by way of turning into the most radical reactions to the historical and the humanistic aspects of the institutions. In his essay 'Naipaul's India And Mine', he becomes violently critical of Naipaul for not adopting an honest and sympathetic relation with the human institution of the subcontinent. Ezekiel takes upon himself the task of defending India against divisive and critical onslaughts of India by Naipaul. In *The Area of Darkness* Naipaul really reaches misonthropic dimensions in being a critic of the primeval states of innocence and ignorance of Indian masses. Ezekiel utterly differs with Naipaul for evolving for himself an unsympathetic critical postures about India and its people. Says Ezekiel:

> *What is destestable is Mr. Naipaul's refusal to see it in human and historic terms.*[7]

But at the same time Ezekiel does not disagree with what all Naipaul has to say about the degraded aspects of human condition in India. Ezekiel in fact compromises with Naipaul, when he says:

> *... I acknowledge without hesitation the existence of all the darkness Mr. Naipaul discovered.*[8]

Ezekiel's retaliation is certainly not against what 'Mr. Naipaul discovered'. In spite of the fact that Naipaul is an expertise Indian, he could not rightly relate himself to India. It is the bitterness of the oppositional spirit in which Naipaul talked of India that ultimately pinches Ezekiel. He wished that Naipaul adopted for himself a more sympathetic view of India in human and historic term. Ezekiel evolves in himself a Typical sympathetic and concerned critic of India, its people, and its institution. For this purpose he considers himself to be the best candidate. Says Ezekiel:

> *I am not a Hindu and my background makes me a natural outsider: circumstances and decisions relate me to India. In other countires I am a foreigner. In India I am an Indian.*[9]

The complacent self-elating manner in which he claims the Indianness is certainly lovable; and being a poet he becomes a sympathetic and concern critic of India and its people. In general almost all the twentieth-century Indo-Anglian poets turned highly critical about the modern India. The expertise writers like Naipaul and Sulman Rushdi found immense material for depicting a degraded picture of Indian culture and society. R. Parthasarathy in his *Indian English Verse; The Making of a Tradition,* exactly diagnosis the minds of Indo-Anglian poets. Say R. Parthasarathy:

> *. . . unable to accept present day India as it is,*
> *and unable to relate themselves comprehend to*
> *traditional India, these poets fall back on irony*
> *to disclose the contradiction inherent in the*
> *Indian situation.*[10]

But, however, Ezekiel's situation is altogether different in spite of the fact that he could not relate himself to the ancestral India, he had immense sympathies for the Indian masses. Moreover, his inherent interest in almost all the major religions of the world like Hinduism, Islam, Judaism and Christianity he developed a compulsion to acquaint himself with all religions. In *My Being Human* (An interview with Nissim Ezekiel, when Frank Birbal Singh asked Ezekiel):

Q. Did you at any stage take an interest in Indian philosophy or religion?

A. Oh, certainly. That started for me at a very early age. I was, after all in a Roman Catholic School, and the Fathers used to say to the students that there was nothing at all in Hinduism. The Hindus, Parsees, Moslems, all said, "What? There is nothing in Hinduism?" So we started reading the *Gita* and *Upanishads* at school, which I may not have done in the next ten years, had the Fathers not said there was nothing in it. I have always felt that substantial truths about life are expressed in Hinduism, Islam, Judaism, Christianity.[11]

It is in his *Latter-Day-Psalms* that we find the best criticism. In being a critic he is extremely sympathetic. Even then he is harshly satirical he does not forget even for a moment his sympathetic concerns for India, and its culture. He always intended to reform Indian people.

Poetic Technique

Humour, irony, paradox and the use of antithesis are the usual traditional ammunitions of criticism and satire. Ezekiel uses all these most discretly and acquires for himself the cradentials of a critic of culture. This property of turning against ones own culture is again the heritage that he acquired from the modern poets. Referring to the critical mode of Nissim Ezekiel Inder Nath Kher says as follows:

> *Comtemplating upon the contemporary human condition, and by focussing on the urban through an ironic mode of perception, Ezekiel seems to be drawing our attention toward the pastoral. I further suggest that Ezekiel's poetry should be viewed as a metaphoric journey into the heart of existence; into the roots of one's self or being which embodies both mythic and existential dimensions of life. This endless quest for meaning and identity intertwined with the search for a poetics, provides Ezekiel with the sense of creative continuity. Through the justaposition of art and life he envisions a state of harmony between the inner and outer landscapes.*[12]

While it is a certain fact that Ezekiel focuses 'on the urban through an ironic mode of perception', he certainly does put draw 'our attention towards the pastoral'. His passion for the premordial experiences of life through instinctive universal apprehensions should not be mistaken as 'attention towards tne pastoral', to the extent that the pastoral in its conventional sense speaks for the primitive life style. The human behaviours here are ruffian with all their primitive and cruel attitudes.

The premordial instinctive perception of Ezekiel is always prompted by his own instinctive apprehensions. With these instinctive apprehensions he rediscovers for himself a sort of personal certainity. He believes, along with T.S. Eliot, that in this world of ideological conclusions the individual is 'needed to work for personal certainity'.[13] It is in this sense that Ezekiel's poetry should be read as a metaphoric journey into the heart of existence. Again Inder Nath Kher is not exactly right in stating that in 'that the roots of one's self or being which embodies both mythic and existential dimensions of life'.[14] While the existential search of Ezekiel is for achieving a personal correspondence by way of juxtaposing inner and outer landscapes of experiences, the very poetic spirit of existential tangle or dilemma in his attempts is to seek a personal certainty of things. The very sympathetic and critical manner with which he looks upon urban is in itself a self-contained metaphoric contradictory mode, which he borrowed from Baudelaire and T.S. Eliot.

As a matter of fact, he is more concerned with the misfortune of poverty, ignorance and helplessness of the masses, rather than with the urbanism itself. It is certainly true that the urban masses are permanently cut-off from the most satisfying report with nature and its rhythms. To that extend the urban man has voluntarily distances himself from the vicinity of nature. As back as 1960, in his poem *Urban* Ezekiel states:

At dawn he never sees the skies
Which, silently, are born again.
Nor feels the shadows of the night
Recline their fingers on his eyes.
He welcomes neither sun nor rain.
His landscape has not depth or height.[15]

The urban agonies are obvious. But then a natural question arises as to what he is stating above is sentimentally exgraded of realistically stated. The urban man anywhere in the world is not literally cut-off from the naturalistic rhythms and modes of life. He often goes for outings and picnics to enjoy the nature's bliss from time to time. Whereas he is part of nature himself his distance from verdure need not be taken as forgetting nature. In a like circumstances Wordsworth writes a poem called *The Gypsies,* wherein he pours forth sentimental tears on the gypsies and their condition of life in not being able to afford a small house for themselves. William Wordsworth momentarily forgets that the gypsies are nomadic tribe which prefers to remain on permanent travel rather than staying in the houses. This kind of sentimental pouring of tears by Wordsworth was critically condemned by John Keats as 'egotistical sublime'. If so what Ezekiel showed in the above poem is not something different, except that it focuses the attention on the urban dwellers. In spite of his sentimentalism Ezekiel becomes clear when he says:

The river which he claims he loves
Is dry, and all the winds lie dead.[16]

The expression which he claims is suggestive of the fact that the urban dwellers could not inherit the 'river' and all its beauties. Again, the expression 'implies' that he is incapable of really loving it. He only affectedly claims the very idea of river is dead and dry for him. On the symbolic plane the river of life is not available for him. The images are quite mari-bound implying that he is living a dead life without the 'mind'. Life giving properties, being in available for him. In spite of all this 'The city like a passion burns.'[17] Even his 'Morning Walk', also are mere dreams. 'And floating on a wave of sand',[18] is also a dream, as though the Bombay beach has become the 'wave of sand'. But then Ezekiel has in mind the hypothetical urban landscape. It may not be exactly Bombay. Even if it is Bombay the sentiments affectedly float far above the fact. As a matter of fact the urban in the case of Ezekiel, as in the case of Baudelaire and T.S. Eliot, is the most convenient metaphor in order to arrive at his personal critical correspondence with the contemporary human condition.

However, the entire poetry of Ezekiel cannot be adjudged as exgraded sentimental metaphors. In fact, after the publication of his *The Unfinished Man* in 1960 Ezekiel was continually searching for appropriate metaphors for his personal experiences. He discovers for himself that all the metaphors, while they are practically convenient materials, are not sufficient for his poetic emotional purpose. In his *A Word For The Wind* he says:

> *I cannot find a word for the wind,*
> *Another word, a phrase full of it*
> *Like a sail.*[19]

In the mean time he realizes the following truth about life. 'Change is permanent and real'.[20] 'Life can be kept alive/

by contact with the unknown and the strange.'[21] Ezekiel further says:

> *Always we must be lovers,*
> *Man and wife at work upon the hard*
> *Mass of materials which is the world,*[22]

Simulatneously his search for metaphor continues:

> *And not in*
> *alcoholic language*
> *but in some needed flame.*[23]

This 'needed flame' is supplied by passion to know. In the inavailability of the desired, the act of knowing becomes a passion for knowledge. Therefore, he says:

> *Speak out*
> *every time and lose*
> *your life to gain it.*[24]

It is a clear indication that you have to be born again and again metaphorically of course, to the ever changing, never resting, change of things around. For this purpose you have to :

> *. . . to burn*
> *your bridges, bury your deed.*[25]

With all this it is just possible that the poet is:

> *Half awakened*
> *he looks again at his*
> *wrong time, wrong place:*[26]

The chief doctrine preached by Ezra Pound was that poetry should use the words and rhythms of natural speech, not only 'specialized diction'. Ezekiel's criticism of the dated and decadent Edwardian style of Aurobindo, reveals his preference for the literary use of colloquial and familiar speech. In *A Time to Change,* he writes:

> *So in our style of verse and life*
> *The oldest idiom may reveal*
> ....
> *Be as original as when the world was made.*[27]

As Harish Raizada states:

> *In this respect Ezekiel belongs to what Northrop Frye calls the 'demotic' tendency in literature. His effort is to minimize the difference between literature and speech, to seek out the associative or prose rhythms that are used in speech and reproduce them in poetry.*[28]

Life is continually floated into continual sequence of lies. Real knowledge never comes. All our search for truth always ends up as a continual discoveries lies one after the other. The death of one is the birth of the other ignorance. This is a sort of a permanent predicament of a poet as a human being. The very title of the poem is *The Poet Comtemplates His Inaction,* not that he is really inactive, he often finds himselfs falling into inappropriate metaphors. That is the existential dilemma and agony of being a poet. That he is not capable of finding an exact and appropriate metaphor, because he always finds himself in wrong time and wrong place'. He has to die every moment and be born again and again, again metaphorically. In spite of the fact that it is a futile exercise, he does not leave that act of trying to find corresponding metaphors for his personal experiences.

Ironic Mode

In the meantime the humour, irony, satire and use of paradox sufficiently convince us that he is continually making personal equations with the world, by way of exposing its incongruities and insufficiencies. In this context the words of P.K.J. Kurup are worth quoting:

> *The predominant feature that strikes the discerning reader of Ezekiel's poetry is his highly private sensibility operating in the context of significant social and ethical changes in independent India. The complexities of contemporary urban existence in India has been his most favourite theme.*[29]

M.H. Williams in his *Indo-Anglian Literature* makes the point much more clear. Says Williams:

> *Many of his poems derive their effectiveness from the poet's puzzled emotional reactions to the modern Indian dilemma which he feels to be poignant conflicts of tradition and modernism, the city and the village. a somewhat obvious theme but treated by Ezekiel as an intensely personal exploration.*[30]

His humour is very very delicate. In never hurts, in spite of his irony is being sharp and slashing like diamond painted arrow. It is worthwhile to analyse the satirical methods and approaches of Ezekiel in order to arrive at his poetic profundity. In the very first poem of his *Sixty Poems* he makes his poetic strategy clear. Say Ezekiel:

I want a human balance humanly
Acquired, fruitful in the common hour.[31]

The expression 'fruitful in the common hour' is very important. The 'common hour' being the shared moments between the poet and his reader, the fruitfulness of the same remains a matter of consciousness correspondence between poet and the reader. Therefore, this balance is 'humanly acquired'. The use of the adverb 'humanly' is implicative of the possible universal ascent for what he suggests as 'human balance'. It is clear indication that he would not be dogmatic in imposing the absurd faiths of people on the readers mind. Says Ezekiel:

Not to seek release but resolution,
Not to hanker for a wide, god-like range
Of thought, nor the matador's dexterity.
I do not want the yogi's concentration.
I do not want the perfect charity
Of saints nor the tyrant's endless power.[32]

The way of the world is full of dogmatic show of proud individual assertions like 'matador s dexterity' and *'yogi's* concentraction' All these faculties are inhumanly acquired and they serve no human purpose

Epistomological Countres

In the very next poem *The Stone* quite paradoxically Ezekiel says:

I have to revel in the stone,
Hard, cold, heavy, shapeless, solid stone,
To turn away from all that seems to flow
Elusively; time, water, blood around the bone

The flare and flux of what is merely show
For something real like a common stone,
Not to be caressed,. like flesh, but hard as bone.[33]

The qualifying objectives that he uses before the like 'hard', 'cold', 'heavy' and 'solid' are understandable but he introduces in between the adjectives shapeless. Like a seasoned symbolist like T.S. Eliot he mystifies the very nature of the stone. Then the stone must a symbol. T.S. Eliot had used it in his *Waste-land* when he said as follows:

There is shadow under this red rock,
(Come in under the shadow of this red rock)
And I will show you something different from either
Your shadow at morning striding behind you
Or your shadow at evening rising to meet you;
I will show you fear in a handful of dust.[34]

In the context of T.S. Eliot the rock symbolically refers to his recently acquired New Anglican faith. Also it is customery in the Catholic Biblical tradition to refer to the Christian religion as a rock and the stone. Ezekiel is certainly not a Catholic or a Christian. But, however, he comes of an old Jewish Orthodox family settled in Bombay; and the jews everywhere in the world acknowledged their faith to the Old Testament of *The Bible.* But, this in itself would not explain Ezekiel's leaning 'revel in the stone'. It is just possible that he is using the image and the symbol of the stone in analogy to T.S. Eliot, but then with a different poetic purpose. In stating the Stone as 'shapeless' he probably means to imply the non-thetic but strongly felt nature of poetry and its power on his mind. Chetan Karnani in his *The Poetry of Nissim Ezekiel: A brief Overview* rightly points out that:

> *It is characteristic of Ezekiel to say that mere warmth of human emotions is not enough unless the heavens grant that greatest gift of genius – the ability to perceive new resemblances.*[35]

If so 'that greatest gift of genius', which has to be granted by 'heavens' is a certain solid consciously felt experience of the poet because of its strong solidly felt nature he prefers poetically to concise it as a stone. 'The Stone' symbol in Ezekiel is certainly not religious faith. It solidly refers to his aesthetic dimensions. This becomes clear in the last three lines of the poem, when Ezekiel says:

> *It does not feel the paralysing flow*
> *Of everything that is not hard as stone*
> *But shares its nature like the hidden bone.*[36]

The 'hidden bone' here stands for the inner solid skeletal structure on which a living being withstand itself. Therefore, quite intriguingly Ezekiel suggests that the form of a poem, with all its organic substantities, is all important for a poet. In this sense it is certainly a bold statement in an age where innumerable experimentations are taking place in the name of liberating the structural dimensions of poems. In a sense he is critical of the moderns who give no great importance for the poetic forms as such.

Most of the poems of Nissim Ezekiel, more particularly *The Unfinished Man,* are epistemological in nature. As K.D. Verma rightly points out that:

> *they (the poems of N. Ezekiel) are mental excursions into some specific aspect or problem of existence.*[37]

The problem here concerns with the ontological faith of Nissim Ezekiel himself in the solid stone like manner in which a poem fabricates itself in his inner authentic self as a solid 'stone'. This is one more important poem on the art of writing poetry. Ezekiel is quite serious here and exposes the credentials of all such modern poets for whom poetic forms are not important at all.

Poetic Experience as a Felt Flow

Nissim Ezekiel certainly makes an experimental permutations and combinations of the free verse forms, but then he affirms that a free verse is certainly not an unbridled linguistic artefact. His love of the time tested traditional forms of poetry is everywhere to see. But, however, he compromises his poetic forms both with the free verse and the traditional verse formulas. However, as he matured in his craft in course of time, he attributed a great importance to the conversational manners of holding the free verse, be way of dramatizing for himself a sort of balance between the internal and the external worlds of experience. He always calls the living experience 'a flow and continuity'; and the poetic worth of this flow is reminiscent upon the moments of expressing the same in a poetical manner. The poetic flow and the flow of life are paralled to each other. This is what he calls the parallelizing flow in the form of the sea. Says Ezekiel:

> *........ the sea*
> *Among its broad realities, attracts*
> *Because it is a symbol of the free*
> *Demoniac life within.*
> *Hardly suggested by the surface facts,*
> *And rivers what a man can hope to win*
> *By simple flowing, learning how to flow,*
> *And trees imply an obvious need of roots,*
> *Besides that all organic growth is slow.*
> *Both poetry and living illustrate:*[38]

Therefore, poetry and living are paralleled and paradoxical properties. In analogy a choice living must necessarily imply a choice report with poetry as an ever continuing, never resting flow of reality. Ezekiel in his poetry is an admirer of the reality of life. When ever this reality gets by passed or subverted by any dogmatic and irrational force, with the help of his ironic mode of perception, he draws our attention towards the possible metaphoric journey into the heart of existence and into the roots of ones self or being. Therefore, Inder Nath Kher sums up Ezekiel's poetic cradentials in a magmaninous manner in the following words. Says Inder Nath Kher :

> *This endless quest for meaning and identity, intertwined with the search for a poetics, provides Ezekiel with the sense of creative continuity.*[39]

Ezekiel's sense of creative continuity is always informed by a relative and equal sensibility of experience in the world of existence. In unifying his sense and sensibility through poetry, he tried his own best to overcome the cultural cleavage, or what the western thinkers designate as Cartasian Dichotomy. Thereby, he tried to overcome that cultural blot, of what T.S. Eliot designates as 'dissociation of sensibility' in his essay on 'The Metaphysical Poets'. This is not to say that Ezekiel could easily come out of the Cartasian Dichotomy. The 'dissociation of sensibility' as a cultural stigma still remains as a reality, because of the inherent distinction between the mind and the matter, between the subjective counters and objective realities of imagination and perception. This is to be found in the artificial styles of life adopted by the people. In his satirical verse Ezekiel substantially exposes the dogmatic artificial properties of life as lived by the people in their grand shows of life, which is shown in his "Poverty Poems."[40] There is a significant note of decent established by Ezekiel towards the materialistic pre-occupation of people in general.

Philosophical Humanism

Nissim Ezekiel cannot be categorized as a philosophical poet, in the sense of making out introspective metaphysical co-relation between God and Man, however, there are innumerable poems which formulate typical self-searching meditative approach comparable to 'Saint Augustan Meditations'. In his philosophical moment he bluntly expresses the agonies of his heart by way of accusing a creator. In this context he is a metaphysical rebel. Referring to his meditative temperament, Vasant A. Shahane in his essay 'The Religious-Philosophical Strain in Nissim Ezekiel's Poerty' says as follows:

> *Ezekiel's post-1967 poems are marked by a strain of what may be described as esthetically inclined philosophical humanism. On the one hand, he is conscious of his own mask, but at the same time he aims 'stripping off a hundred veils' of creation and the creator. His theological position has to be stated in purely humanistic terms. In this philosophical system aimed at restructuring man's relationship with God, Society and Nature Ezekiel expresses his own inner response: 'Lord, I am tired/of being wrong.' This feeling of metaphysical exhaustion alternates with a realization that God's truth is too important and great for man and, therefore, it cannot be brought within the narrow framework of utilitarian objective:*[41]

In the created world of God there is always a certain insufficiency which prompts Ezekiel to rebel at the divinity. Says Ezekiel:

> *Your truth*
> *is too momentous for man*
> *and not always useful.*[42]

In a very humorous manner he tries to effect a compromise with God by way of asking him to consider his prayer seriously. Says Ezekiel:

> *O well, if you insist,*
> *I'll do your will.*
> *Please try to make it coincide with mine.*[43]

This kind of meditative strain is to be found in his *Poster Prayers.* There in, he successfully articulates his selves metaphysical grievances. Ezekiel himself considered that he found his real voice in these poems. Says Ezekiel:

> *The prayers, I feel, are in my true voice, even when not poetry of a high or even moderately high order. They embody all his distinctive attitudes and values, I consider the Poster Poems and the Poster Prayers, taken together, as a suitable expression of a phase in my poetic career. I would be less happy if something of this kind had not happened to me.*[44]

In this later poems Ezekiel's divided nature of his earlier poems gets compromised into a unified approach of a thinker towards life.

In all the poetry of Ezekiel there is a spacious self-acknowledge commitment towards culture, towards fellowmen and towards his own self as a poet. This aspect of Nissim Ezekiel is taken up for analysis in the preceding chapter.

REFERENCES

1. K.R. Srinivasa Iyengar, *Indian Writing in English* (New Dehi: Sterling Publishers Pvt. Ltd., 1989), p. 643.
2. P. Lal, 'An Arrival in Indo-Anglian Poetry', *The Alien Insiders: Essays on Indian Writing in English* (Calcutta: A Writers Workshop Book, 1987), p. 86.
3. David MuCutchion, 'Examen De Midi', *Indian Writing in English* (Calcutta: A Writers Workshop, 1969), p. 118.
4. Inder Nath Kher, ed., *Journal* of *South Asian Literature,* Vol. XI, Nos. 3-4 (Spring, Summer 1976), p. 17.
5. D.J. Enright & E.D. Chickera, eds., *English Critical Texts: 16th Century to 20th Centuries,* (London: Oxford University Press, 1962), p. 180.
6. Inder Nath Kher, ed., *Journal* of *South Asian Literature* Vol. XI, Nos. 3-4 (Spring, Summer 1976), p. 193.
7. *Ibid.,* p. 199.
8. *Ibid.,* p. 202.
9. *Ibid.,* p. 203.

10. R. Parthasarathy, 'Indian English Verse: The Making of a Tradition', *Alien Voice: Perspective on Commonwealth Literature*, ed Avadhesh Shrivastava, (Lucknow: Print House Publishers, 1981), p. 52.
11. Frank Birbal Singh, 'My Being Human: An Interview with Nissim Ezekiel', *Contemporary Indian English Poetry*, ed. Atma Ram, (Calcutta: A Writers Workshop Publication, 1989), p. 181.
12. Inder Nath Kher, ed., *Journal* of *South Asian Literature*, Vol. XI Nos. 3-4 (Spring, Summer 1976), p. 4.
13. Nina Baym, ed., *The Norton Anthology* of *American Literature* (New York: N.W. Norton & Co., 1986).
14. Inder Nath Kher, ed., *Journal* of *South Asian Literature*, Vol. XI, Nos. 3-4 (Spring, Summer 1976), p. 4.
15. *Ibid.*, p. 61.
16. Nissim Ezekiel, *Latter-Day Psalms* (Delhi : Oxford University Press, 1982), p. 58.
17. *Ibid.*, p. 58.
18. *Ibid.*, p. 58.
19. Inder Nath Kher, ed., *Journal of South Asian Literature*, Vol. XI, Nos. 3-4, (Spring, Summer 1976), p. 18.
20. *Ibid.*, p. 21.
21. *Ibid.*,
22. *Ibid.*, p. 23.
23. *Ibid.*, p. 152.
24. *Ibid.*,
25. *Ibid.*,
26. *Ibid.*,
27. Nissim Ezekiel, *A Time to Change* (London: Fortune Press, 1952).
28. Harish Raizada, 'Nissim Ezekiel's Poetry of Love and Sex', *Living Indian English Poets*, ed. Madhusudan Prasad, (New Delhi: Sterling Publishers Pvt. Ltd., 1989), p. 105.
29. P. K. J. Kurup 'Voyage': The Self in the Poetry of Nissim Ezekiel, *Contemporary Indian Poetry in English* (New Delhi: Atlantic Publishers and Distributors, 1991), pp. 11 & 12.
30. H.M. Williams, *Indo-Anglian Literature: 1800-1970* (Bombay: Orient Longman, 1976), p. 118.

31. Nissim Ezekiel, *Sixty Poems* (Bombay: Ekveera Printers, 1953), p. 1-3.
32. *Ibid.*, p. 3.
33. *Ibid.*, p. 4.
34. Michael Roberts, ed., *The Faber Book of Modern Verse* (London Faber and Faber Ltd., 19665), p. 92.
35. Inder Nath Kher, ed., *Journal* of *South Asian Literature,* Vol. XI, Nos. 3-4, (Sprtng, Summer 1976), p. 224.
36. Nissim Ezekiel, *Sixty Poems* (Bombay : Ekveera Printers, 1953), p. 4.
37. Inder Nath Kher ed., *Journal of South Asian Literature,* Vol. XI, Nos. 3-4 (Spring, Summer 1976), p. 230.
38. Nissim Ezekiel, *Sixty Poems* (Bombay: Ekveera Printers, 1953), p. 3.
39. Inder Nath Kher, ed., *Journal of South Asian Literature,* Vol. XL Nos. 3-4 (Spring, Summer 1976), p. 4.
40. Nissim Ezekiel, *Latter-Day Psalms* (Delhi: Oxford University Press, 1982), p. 13.
41. Inder Nath Kher, ed., *Journal of South Asian Literature,* Vol, XI, Nos. 3-4 (Spring, Summer 1976), p. 254.
42. *Ibid.,*
43. Nissim Ezekiel, *Hymns is Darkness* (Delhi: Oxford University Press, 1976), p. 49.
44. Inder Nath Kher, ed., *Journal of South Asian Literature,* Vol. XI, Nos. 3-4 (Spring, Summer 1976), p. 264.

4

Nissim Ezekiel's Social Commitment

From the point of view of progressive maturity of thought and social criticism, the following poetical collections of Ezekiel are very Important:

1. *A Time to Change* (1952).
2. *The Unfinished Man* (1960).

As he himself stated many of these poems have a salient curative dimensions. While the romantic idealism of Ezekiel reaches its height in these poems, there is simultaneous emergence of criticism and exposure of the shames and disgraces of Indian life. Says Ezekiel:

> *Scores of my poems, are obviously written for, personal, therapeutic purpose.*[1]

The word 'therapeutic' here refers to exulting creative operations, as well as for healing act. Both these meanings are significantly applicable. This is amply illustrated in a number of poems in his *A Time to Change*. His well-known poem *Enterprise* is an example here.

The very theme of the poem concerns with a pilgrimage

undertaken with all hopes and dreams. A journey in Christian mythological tradition is a spiritual act. According to the *Bible,* the original home of man is in the heaven, and spiritually speaking, his life on the earth is a transitory phase, which is final goal in reaching heaven by following Jesus Christ. At time the spiritual struggle in journey drops on the way, and various other differences characterize the poem with a sustained note of melancholic nostalgia. When the final destination is reached the glamour and enthusiasm of the adventure itself becomes a frustrating experience. All the idealistic efforts turn to be an exercise in futility. This is the way that Ezekiel introduces the existential note in his poetry:

> *When, finally, we reached the place,*
> *We hardly knew why we were there.*[2]

A common experience to all who dream and fight, to turn the dream into the reality. It is interesting to note that the poem *Enterprise* starts in a parallel relation to T.S. Eliot's poem '*Journey of the Magi*'.[3] While the *Journey of Magi* bears a close knit parallelism to the biblical journey of three kings called the Magi to the place of nativity of the son of God, Ezekiel's poem is quite secular in its proposition. The journey motive itself has a copious reference to the tourist interest. But, however, on the symbolic and suggestive plane the poem ultimately refers to the futility and fruitlessness of the journey of life. The poem itself maintains certain conspicuous echoes to W.B. Yeats' melancholic nostalgia. The fruitlessness of the imaginative journey to the romantic Byzantium becomes evident in 'Yeats' Byzantium poems'.[4] It is therefore important to note that Ezekiel is envasaging here the potential strands of the two major British poets of the modern times. The very poetic perfection of Ezekiel lies in the ingenious manner in which he followed the footsteps of the great masters. Ezekiel comes to a conclusion that all the poets who dream and fight and who wish to turn the dream into a reality are invariably fated to frustration. This is so because 'dream and reality' stand as veritable parallel opposites of approach in life. But, however the romantic temper of Ezekiel, as prompted by the British romantic poets, invariably lands him into an unending struggle and fight, the note of frustration and struggle shown here is obviously sweet, because of its imaginative idealistic heights.

It is a rare distinction on the part of Nissim Ezekiel that he perennially aspired simultaneously to capture the romantic heights of the British Romantics and the realistic note of the moderns. Structurally speaking *Enterprise* is a sweet and significant vocal performance in which he captures the speech rhythm of the colloquial English. *A Time to Change* significantly brings forth his poetic colloquial maturity. P. Lal in his 'An Arrival in Indo-Anglian Poetry' says as follows:

> *Mr. Nissim Ezekiel is, I think, one of our better poets because he is the most consistent in maintaining a happy balance between experiment in technique and the introspective urge. Now and then the balance is replaced by a fusion, and the result is a memorable poem.*[5]

Ezekiel's manner of 'maintaining a happy balance between experiments in technique and introspective urge' is a definite poetic achievement. But, all his experiments in technique are close knit and faithful formalistic analogical renderings for the British poets. It is not to say that they are slavishly imitative. But, it is certainly assertive of the fact that Ezekiel produces certain charming analogical parallel to those of the British poets. Imitation in itself is a matter of slavish adoptation. But creating an analogy, that too a poetic one, is a matter of artistic achievement in being a creative (or recreative) act of performance in language. According to Wallace Stevens 'all poetry is a profound analogy for life'.[6] If so, an analogy for another poem, which in itself is a perfect analogy of life, ultimately becomes an analogy of life itself. It is not imitation; it is re-creation.

Episodic Structure

Immediately after a few lines subsequent to the above quotation, P. Lal makes quite a depressing statement about Ezekiel's poetry. Says P. Lal:

> *There could be no more misleading title as an introduction to his poetry. There is really no notion of change in these poems, at least no change in the sense of the poet moving from one stage into another, or of development of one idea into another. There is movement, but not change; growth, but not paradoxically development.*[7]

P. Lal is probably taken away by the ordinary review makers, rhetoric of resorting to effected use of verbal antithesis. It is not right to say 'there is really no notion of change' in these poems. P. Lal prefers to blind-fold himself to the progressively maturing analogies, of poetic forms here. According to Ezekiel a poem is something more than an episode. These more than episodic dimensions of poetry are obviously present here. The situational exactness of a realistic incident is very much present in every poem. But the episode itself forms part of one great poem called the life of man. The particular incident in a poem clings to life as a casual and natural entanglement to general human life, with all its aspirations. The following lines are an example of point:

> *It is the way,*
> *The how, the what, the flow*
> *From which a poem comes,*
> *In which the savage and the singular,*
> *The gentle, familiar,*
> *Are all dissolved the residue*
> *Is what you read, as a poem, the rest*
> *Flows and is poetry.*
> *This should be so, Precisely so.*[8]

After all the material particulars are assembled in the poem. The final outcome should be somewhat a changing poetic pattern in whose absorption there is that heighest poetic experience. Therefore, Ezekiel says 'after all the poetic form dissolves'. The formal texture that we read is only a 'poem'. The essential spirit of enjoyment what we call 'poetry' is what it is to be found in experiencing self, as a form of enjoyment. Therefore, Ezekiel says, 'the rest flows and is poetry'. The formula of enjoyment that Ezekiel attributes to poetic experience is what the modern psychologists call the *Aha-experience* in aesthetics. This *aha-experience* is the final criteria of judging poetry as form of art. In fact, the poem is different from poetry in being a skeletal assemblage of material particulars of structuralizing a poem. The aim of achieving the state of poetry gets achieved if only that *aha-experience* is successfully created.

Personal Sensibility

The categorical distinction that Ezekiel makes between poem and poetry becomes clear in the following words of Wallace Stevens:

> *A poem is a poem, not because it is a poem,*
> *but because of its personal experience.*[9]

These ideas of W. Stevens are significantly anchored by Ezekiel in the, above lines.

Ezekiel's poetic idealism apply conforms itself to the above ideas of Wallace Stevens insistence on 'personal sensibility' as 'the medium of poetry'. It suggests that a poem as a compact structure is only a manner of expressing that personal sensibility. Poetry as a profound flow surges out of that 'personal sensibility'. As such poetry *per se* (is somethings more than the poem as a structure. The same idea is reflected by Ezekiel in the following lines; which have been discussed before, but it is worth quoting again: Says Ezekiel:

> *It is the why*
> *The how, the what, the flow*
> *From which a poem comes,*
> *In which the savage and the singular,*
> *The gentle, familiar,*
> *All are dissolved. the residue*
> *Is what you read, as a poem, the rest*
> *Flows and is poetry.*
> *This should be so, Precisely so.*[10]

'The flow metaphor' through which 'the why', 'the how' and 'the what' emerge themselves to form into a poem is the structure of the poem. It is into this 'the savage and the singular', the 'gentle', 'familiar' are all dissolved. The contingent effect is characterised by Ezekiel as 'the rest'. It is that 'rest' that 'flows is poetry'. 'The savage and the singular' refers to the primeval 'personal sensibility', which is always unique in being a particular of personal experience. The extra affirmation that he adds in stating 'this should be so, precisely so' shows the authentic manner in which he holds the poetry in the highest order of art. P. Lal quotes the last stanza of Ezekiel's poem *Creation* to confirm this romantic ideal of Ezekiel:

> *Child of flesh and fancy,*
> *Be equable, as the sages recommend,*
> *And God-like make a universe*
> *Of fire, and flesh, and air, and water.*[11]

While the expression 'the child of flesh' refers to the instinctive sensibility of man, the 'fancy' aspect of it refers to the divine inspiration as held by Holdorlin. In stating that both are 'equable' (be equable) Ezekiel's devotion for personal sensibility becomes explosive. The point becomes clear in the expression 'the sages recommend'. He further escort the poet to be exactly 'God-like' and make a 'universe of fire, and flesh, and air and water'. The elemental manner, of performance substantiates the divine inspirational aspect of his poetic genious.

But this kind of the divine inspirational aspect of poetry is only a chance inspired content of Ezekiel's poems very sparingly used. Otherwise Ezekiel, as a poetic a critical realist. As a critical realist most of his poems turn out to be concerned ironic 'reflections of the unfortunate state of human existence in the world of material abundances. The material abundances as higher material comforts achieved by man are not exactly preferable for his poetic temperament. They are far below the reality of poetic manner of understanding man and matter.

It becomes evident that Ezekiel's poetic personality is a divided self. As an inspired poet he upholds the divinity, and as a critical realist he denounces human tendencies. He exactly deplores the cut and dry practical manner in which people prefer to live their lives by way of exclusively indulging in the pleasures of flesh. The world should have long refused to be corrupted by the dreadful and unbecoming models of life. Modern day life is perennially preoccupied by:

Newspapers, cinemas, radio features, speeches
Demanding peace by men with grim warlike faces
Posters selling health and happiness in bottles,
Large returns for small investments, in football pools
Or self-control, six easy lessons for a pound,
Holidays in Rome for writing praise of tooth pastes. . .[12]

The 'insidious net of the flesh' (to borrow the expression of P. Lal), it all exactly is in opposition to the world of fancy or imanigation of a poet. Therefore, Ezekiel prefers to relegate himself to the idea of absorbing himself into a poetic world of experience in which all the questions, all the doubts, and all the wonders become extinguished. Says Ezekiel:

There shall be no more question,
No more expenditure of doubt
but only a limpid style of life
Whose texture is poetry.[13]

He admits that all the styles of life as absorbed in day-to-day life are corrupt. But, a poet should be able to elevate himself from this corrupt life by way of attributing for it a 'tempted style', 'whose texture is poetry'. The quick flux-like signification manner of practical life, when sanctified by personal sensibility, turns out to be a glorious personal and unique property, whose flow emerges the poet into joy. All this vehemently testifies the fact that the poet should live the monotonous dead and lonely life as lived by the people around him; but he should be able to look at them with a sense of objectivity, which in itself provides for him what he calls the 'limpid style of life'. Different people have different ideas and conceptions of what constitutes a happy life. As a matter of fact happiness itself is a matter of a transitory interior phenomena, an ever changing formula which conforms with the expression 'limpid'. In order to achieve a poetic temper and passion, he does not want to become a sage and renounce the world. But, at the same time he does not want to be crossed by the day-to-day life material. He only wants to convert the entire material of observation into a formula of getting absorbed into the true social texture of life. In the very first poem *A Time to Change,* Ezekiel makes it clear:

Perception in April
Of my condition
Secret faults concealed no more.
Withdrawn to look

At my condition
Secret faults concealed no more.
A lighter touch
A smoother line
Excesses cut
Simplicity
And Secret faults concealed no more.
The going forth
Prepared with prayer
The timed return
Redeemed with prayer.[14]

Temper and Temperament

Nissim Ezekiel's critical temper and temperament is born of his frustration with the primitive and backward state of various institutions. The Indian traditional institutions being orthodox and back looking in their approach to life are highly uncongenial for the establishment of freedom and choice by individuals. Adding to the backwardness to the Indian social institutions, the new Western cultural courses of life and that touched the continent turned the people of the country into an ignorant crowds pursuing lazy and purposeless lives. Very often because of their backwardness the people fail to under stand the niceties of co-existence, may it be in the family or in the society at large. In this context the words of P.S. Kasture in his essay 'The Nature of Chaos in Modern Indo-Anglian Poetry' is worth quoting. Says P.S. Kasture that Nissim Ezekiel's poetry:

> *is not a positive affirmation but an attempt to come to terms with darkness. This conscious confrontation of chaos does not lead him to nothingness, but being aware of the*

> *facts of life and death, Ezekiel sees through*
> *all sham consolations and ultimately a sense of*
> *reality sorges in his mature mind.*[15]

The ultimate sense of reality that 'surges in his mature mind', concerns with the poetic manner in which he comprehend social reality.

It is all certainly true that India is a land of many cultures and many traditions, but people as such, very often fore-close themselves from being prime member of a civilized society. What all Ezekiel wanted is a sort of pleasant understanding between the people with reason and emotion standing together in equal balances. But very often people are found to be more emotional and less reasonable in their attitudes towards nature, towards fellowman, and even towards themselves. Needless to say that happiness, which should have been a reasonable free gift of nature permanently, alludes them. This is because of the widespread ignorances and refusal to consider others as equal individuals, with equal dignities of life. Indians very often are led away by their local loyalties to their own creeds and classes, and their creeds and clans are nurtured by inauthentic emotions. The following lines make Ezekiel's point very clear:

> *Let reason and emotion fare*
> *As man and wife; let them quarrel*
> *Make love or live occasionally*
> *Apart, and then be reconciled,*
> *But let them not, in indifferently,*
> *Empty the house of words and music,*
> *Partners of a marriage in decay. . .*[16]

Balance between Sense and Sensibility

It was the British metaphysical poet John Donne, who always wanted a typical balance of reason and emotion in a given situation in an individual. This according to Donne is a prerequisite for happiness. T.S. Eliot, in his own way conforms the equation into a needful report between sense and sensibility. Likewise, Ezekiel speaks of a perfect blending between reason and emotion, 'they both should fare as man and wife'. The metaphor is quite intriguing. He accepts that they both are warring partners in a given individual but the war should remain at state of a lover's quarrel. Both reason and emotion in a given individual should not become indifferent towards each other. If such indifferent onsets is in an individual there is nothing to say or nothing to enjoy. This empties 'the house of words and muse', that is to say that life becomes a typical conservatory of nothingness. There is neither scope for expression through language nor enjoyment through singing lives content in ecstasy. This state of affairs Ezekiel calls marriage in decay; and 'reason' and 'emotion' are the partners in it. The marriage partners metaphor for 'reason' and 'emotion' is also due to the poetic influence of John Donne and his other metaphysical followers. This is perhaps a very reasonable demand on the part of the poet. But it certainly is not achievable as early as said. His little vision of life very often gets distorted because of the simple reason that the establishment of balance between reason and emotion is not possible at all. A rackless disregard for the basic disciplines of life is at the root of the misery of the Indians. Ezekiel's authentic meditation and the mystical advice that he gives are arresting in this context. Says Ezekiel:

The way of speech is difficult
To find and the way of silence is
Difficult to find.
Trust the way
My son, that is difficult to find.[17]

In a way both 'the way of speech and the way of silence' are difficult. There is nothing left to talk or discuss about life. Therefore, the real creed that he proposes for man of God is that man who implicity puts a faith in the mystery of God, therefore, Ezekiel writes as follows:

To own a singing voice and a talking voice,
A bit of land, a woman and a child or two
Accomodated to their needs and changing moods,
And patiently to build a life with these;
A bit of land, a woman and a child or two
Accomodated to their needs and changing moods,
Practising and singing and a talking voice
Is all the creed a man of God requires.
He has to build something with able hands
And knowing eyes, with some instructions
From his parents, ancestors and friends
Altered slightly here and there to suit his
strength.
He has to silence no one but himself
And walk occasionally on alien land
To know the various lives and dreams of men,
And show his deep affection for the world
With words emerging from a contrite heart.[18]

He advices all the simplicities of life for a decent and dignified manner of existing in the world. While a 'singing voice' refers to ones own personality. The 'talking voice' refers to that of his partner in life. This is the minimum prerequisite for happy life. The rest to follow is 'a bit of land', etc., etc., but all this, one has to achieve by himself. 'He has to build something with able hands'. It is this ability of hand that speaks for the real heroism in man. The dignity of being human gets established. It is the lack of this dignity of being human that eats away the very marrow of Indian social system. Therefore, he looks upon the system with a sense of disgust and unease. This is the kind of change and alteration that he wants in the attitude and disposition of man. This exactly is the message of his collection *A Time to Change.*

The Necessary Change

In the true manner of the modern British and American romantics like W.B. Yeats and Wallace Stevens, Ezekiel wants man to start afresh his sincere adventure of life by way of converting himself into a primitive or a savage. The superstructure of social, cultural and moral life of man in the world should invariable start in this assumption of primitivie within the given contexts of the social and cultural properties there is no way of compromising reason and emotion as his 'hymnical partners'. The only way left out for man is to discord all that is given to him in the name of civilization. Only then he can think of assigning proper places in himself for reason and emotion. Lack of balance between reason and emotion forms part of the thesis of his latter publication *The Unfinished Man.*

In the Indian social and cultural situation Ezekiel finds a sort of unbridgeable cleavage (gulf) between senses and emotions. The categorical pictures of the Indian man and woman as drawn by Ezekiel about in this cleavage, as a result of which the characters appears incongruous, ironic and grossly humorous. In all the humorous and ironic portraits of the poet there is frustration and cynicism underlying in the characters. They are the mocking pictures of progress and self-assumed heights and prerogatives. The antithetical formulas of human disposition between the past and the present, are given with a sense of disgust. The following makes the point clear. Says Ezekiel:

> *'Love was high minded, stable'*
> *But now on the other hand*
> *'Now he wears a thicker*
> *skin, upgraded from*
> *the goddesses of virtue*
> *to mocking, sexual eyes*
> *whose hanger makes him wise.'*[19]

Since the protagonist of the poem 'wears thicker skin, upgraded from goddesses of virtue, and resorts to mocking sexual eyes', the fallenness of the person is obvious, and his hunger for flesh obviously makes him a typical modern character. The hunger of the 'mocking sexual eyes' making him wise is quite ironic and speaks for the lack of personal values and dignities. The same kind of mocking tone and ironic profundity prevails all through his poetry. The theme of his poem *Healers* is as follows:

> *It does not matter*
> *if you cannot love your wife.*
> *It does not matter*
> *if your marriage is arranged.*
> *It does not matter*
> *if you teach or advertise.*
> *God's love remains your heritage.*
> *You need not change*

your way of life.
Know your mantra, meditate,
release your kundalini,
get your shakti awakening and float with the
spirit to your destination.[20]

God-man, spiritual healers, and quacks are very common in India. Even after the advent of the most scientific medical equipments and doctors an average citizen of India usually consults these quacks, God-man and spiritual healers. Their prescriptions are out and out laughable are irrational and incapable of offering any real cure. While these realizing *kundalini* is a *yoga* to be achieved after a vigorous imitation into yogic practices. The spiritual healer offers the advice as though it is very easy to perform. But, any way, this is the kind of unbecoming advices that are given by quacks and spiritual healers. They are flourishing simply because of innocence and ignorance, coupled with an extreme conservative attitudes of the people at large.

In his poem *Servant* Ezekiel expresses one more sinister point of Indian life. Orunkness amongst the male members of the lower masses is the widest phenomena in the Indian life. Here is the sad story of a maid-servant. The maid-servant comes to work at 6 a.m. and works day and day. Then at nineteen she is married to a brute. Says Ezekiel:

...... and tells my mother every time
her husband beats her
for the fun of it. (21)

There are two vital brutal aspect of Indian society exposed here. Her coming to work at 6 a.m. and working day and day out as a child labour is one; and the other concerns are painful-domestic life in her marriage. Drunkenness coupled with sadness or some other deep rooted psychological melody is the cause of her husband beating 'her for the fun of it'. But in a very intelligent manner Ezekiel exposes the unpercieved sadness usually catered to the domestic servant by the comfortable masters too in the society. The poet's mother tells him about the maid-servant's unfortunate state of affair, probably assuming upon herself a sort of false and affected sympathies. She speaks as though she knows pleasantly the brutal stories about the world, by way of suggesting that this is the most brutal of all. Says the mother:

> *I am absorbed in news*
> *of brutal stories brought*
> *to my breakfast table*
> *from every corner*
> *of the Godless world.*[22]

The mother getting 'absorbed in news of brutal stories brought to her breakfast table fresh from every corner of the Godless world', refers to the newspapers which bring forth all disgusting information concerning accidents, violent deaths, suicides, etc. The complacent manner in which the mother disperses the stream of the burden of the news to 'the Godless world' is quite ironic and intriguing. It is just possible that mother takes a psychological vicarious pleasure in absorbing herself 'in news of brutal stories'. It all speaks for her scandal mongering instinct, which is very common in the Indian folks. In this context the words of P.P. Mehta are particularly important. Says Mehta:

> *We have eyes for brutality at large but we are too shortsighted to see brutality at home. A sad comment on our social structure !*[23]

Looked from this most common brutality angle the poem *Servant* is not as horrific as 'Yeshwant Jagtap'. The poem tells the story of a hand-cart pusher. He lives in a slum hut. When the rainwater force through the root the entire family perches on a cot. In the rain, water in adds the floor of the hut to the height of the cot. He also places his child on his shoulder where he has learnt to sleep. He keeps himself awake. Ezekiel's end comment is really heart burning:

> *A true-blue Indian be*
> *is reconciled to his lot*
> *and so are we.*[24]

Ezekiel does not fare anyone in India from this thick skinned brutality of perfection, of brutality towards fellow humans, speaks of man's injustice towards his fellowman, tolerance and lip sympathy paid on to such widespread brutality in the society speaks only a far deep water melody in the Indian polity.

Exploitation Being a Way of Life

The brutality aspect of the Indians is not limited to the poverty-stricken masses. The most sophisticated gentry of the city too is free from that. Ezekiel's poem *Hangover* makes the point clear. There are two complimentary pictures of the city night drawn in the poem. On the one hand, this is a posh hotel bar, dance and expensive menu, intellectual discussions, and multi-children families eating over rich food. Closely contested with, we have the drunken pavement sleepers, and the last train to Borivili with two blind beggars, husband and wife in the first class compartment. Ezekiel's authentic feeling about all this is that this is a great incongruity in the lives of city people. In the first picture the vanities and gluttonous are obvious. In the second picture there is the irony of blind beggars travelling in the first class compartment. The most important thing to reckon with in the context of the poem concerns with the uncomfortable and disgusting personal feelings of the poet. He does not approve of lives of people whether they are rich or poor. The scenes of riches and poverty simultaneously prick the conscience of the poet. He expresses his personal feelings of rebellion in the most unapproving manner of making caricatures of life styles. The words of P. P. Mehta are worth quoting in this context:

> *Such scenes of poverty, disease and soullessness are usually contrasted with posh hotel scenes, Goan Christian boys celebrating the new year. Anglo-Indian boys, and Indian well to do families aping the western fashions.*[25]

Poetic Experience

Needless to say that the emotions here are packed into a rebellious expression. They are not direct expressions of emotions. Cleanth Brooks and R.P. Warren in their book *Understanding Poetry* contend that 'emotional expression is an essential element of poetry'.[26] At the same time he further states that:

> *We have feelings and attitudes* concerning *the world of action, just as we have them concerning ideas; and poetry, we may add, does not treat feelings and attitudes except as they come specifically into expression that is, as they come into the realm of action and ideal.*[27]

Feelings coming 'into the realm of action and ideas' is a matter of the poet undergoing a personal experience of the emotions through the feelings represented. A poem really taken its living quality when it exactly personalizes feelings and ideas by way of rendering them into expressed ideas Ezekiel also in his *Ideas and Modern Poetry*, expresses the same opinion:

> *Perhaps it is true then that in good poetry ideas appear not only as ideas but as the poet's experience of those ideas in the best modern poetry we encounter ideas of this nautre, often reflecting current ideas in the social, political and philosophical spheres, but expressing, as Eliot once put it, what it feels like to have those ideas.*[28]

S.N. Prasad substitutes the word 'cognitions' for the word 'ideas' very pertinently. The following words of S.N. Prasad clarify the point:

> *We may replace the word "ideas" used by Cleanth Brooks, R.P. Warren and Nissim Ezekiel with "congnitions" and say that cognitions truly shape the content of poetry only when what it feels like to have those cognitions.*[29]

Prasad's whole contention is that:

> *... the poetic self in Ezekiel has undergone a sort of consecration at cognitive level.*[30]

The expression 'consecration at cognitive level' is very important. This is so because the ideas and the feelings while implanting the discoverable a cognitive level of understanding, the ideas themselves undergo a sort of purification by way of becoming arrestingly novel in their effect on the readers mind. Thereby, a graphic new experience gets enveloped. The same point is poetically comprehended by Ezekiel in his poem *Poetry Reading*. Ezekiel says that when the poet reads his poems:

> *An image fell*
> *Like silver coin upon the floor,*
> *We listed to its echo swell*
> *That message from another shore*
> *Where he, released from worldly things,*
> *Was dumb before the sight he saw.*[31]

This is precisely what it happens to readers in the poems of Ezekiel. All this looks as though a 'message from another shore', that another shore being the packed emotional expressions of the poet in the realm of action and ideas. The pictures of life of the city as given by Ezekiel are not something new. But, the manner in which the poet goes and under goes his personal experience is very important. It is such personal experiences of the poet for whom the ordinary people have become almost immune in their capacity to percieve their ghostly nature. This immunity in the public emerges because of their own exclusive preoccupation with their problems of life. Again as S.T. Coleridge would like to put it:

> *"...We have eyes, yet see not, ears that hear not, and hearts that neither feel nor understand.*[32]

Ezekiel's poems are easy conversational renderings of the widespread ghostliness and squarrose of the city life written for all such readers who have no eyes to see and ears to hear.

This kind of undergoing a personal experience is a matter pain for the poet himself. He is neither comfortable nor he indulges in heart rending scandals by way of giving an expression to such nesty dimensions of life in a city. In his poem, *In India* he sufficiently expresses the poet's painfulness in undergoing such personal process of experience. Writes Ezekiel:

> *Here among the beggars,*
> *Hawkers, pavement sleepers,*
> *Hutmen dwellers, slums,*
> *Dead souls of men and gods,*
> *Burnt-out mothers, frightened*
> *Virgins, wasted child*
> *And tortured animal,*
> *All in noisy silence*
> *Suffering the place and time,*
> *I ride my elephant of thought,*
> *A Cezanne slung around my neck.*[33]

In the above lines Ezekiel critical realism and his romantic and idealism go and hand in hand. The poet riding 'my elephant of thought' is certainly reminiscent of romantic nostalgia and the erruption of melancholy out of reflecting on himself and his helpless situation. He is not free to separate himself from this reflexive self turning against himself. His own imaginative performance and his manner of associating the objective reality of the world is in itself a sort of painful experience. Therefore, it is a 'Cezanne slung around my neck'. Referring to this poem Christopher Wiseman in his Essay 'The Development of Technique in the Poetry of Nissim Ezekiel' says as follows:

> *. . .highly effective in combining its formal,*
> *romantic literary echoes with the satirical*
> *colloquial content.*[34]

In his poem *The Neutral* Nissim Ezekiel becomes more colloquially vocal about his precedent as a poet. This kind of drastic division between the mind's prerequisite of a comfortable romantic imagination sharply cut into drastic objective and the real aspects of life becomes a very natural phenomenal sequence of thought and imagination in the poet. Says Ezekiel:

> *I signed the mainfesto*
> *I paid the subscription*
> *I worked on the committee*
> *I attended the party*
> *It made no difference*
> *The common language*
> *hid my absence.*[35]

The Audensque agony of the poet in realizing that all his heights as a human and the dignity of being human automatically converge into hateful and heinous aspects. As it is natural that the man is always submerged by the common placeness or the degradedness of being human in a society or culture that cannot offer any heights or elevations it is in itself a formula of pain. The common language hiding 'my absence' is quite an intriguing manner of using antithesis for a poetic effect. The common language or day-to-day experience expressed through common language swallows his total identity by way of declaring man a useless non-entity. The common place hiding his absence is reflective of the aesthetic nature of life in swallowing up all the imaginative heights of being in the world. The next stanza clarifies his point of view more clearly:

> *Customer*
> *in the shop of the world*
> *tourist from another planet*
> *citizen of past or future*
> *deceiving with appearances*
> *passing as a human being.*[36]

He calls himself Customer, in the shop of the world'.[6] It is reflective of the most business like lack-luster properties of human relations. He also calls himself as a 'tourist from another planet', implying that he is finding the entire scenario of life in its matter of fact dimensions as a stranger. He is not at home having divided the stream of life between the past and the future with the present being in available. The poetic sentiment here is reminiscent of T.S. Eliot's initiation of the *Waste-land*:

> *April is the cruellest month, breeding*
> *Lilacs out of the dead land, mixing*
> *Memory and desire,*[37]

While the 'memory' part refers to the 'past', the 'desire' part refers to 'future'. This implies that human state is divided between the past and the future in such a painful manner that the present in which we live is altogether eclipsed. In this world of ours, with its testing imagination 'A Cezanne slung around my neck' man never finds himself at home. Living here and now is permanently denied to him. He had to decieve himself 'with appearances', as the reality of the world never becomes available for him, Therefore, he is 'passing as a human being', which in itself is a sad reflection on the state of life of man. Human fulfilments never come to him in his natural state of existence. He has to take upon himself that honourable privilege of human being, while he just plays the mere dramatic roles in life. Therefore, says Ezekiel:

Making love to many women
as to the same women,
playing father, uncle, son, nephew,
brother, cousin, x-in-law,
changing jobs, roles, gods,
virtues, vices, points of view,
courageous-cowardly and callous-sensitive
between the doubtful words and silences.[38]

Life Being a Fiction

All the role models of life are ultimately the fictions created by language. Otherwise being human is just a matter of assuming silence on oneself. Since we do not know exactly what is being human, we take an easy and chance recourse to the various role models of being in the world. These role models as confectioned by language do not give us the ultimate satisfactions. Therefore, Ezekiel's observation is exactly right in designating our state to have been divided 'between the doubtful words and silences'. Ezekiel is reflecting the tragic sentiments of the modern American writers like U.G. O'Neill and Tennesse

Williams. Their life work reflects the idea that 'the greatest tragedy of man is his exclusive dependence on language in his search for truth'. Ezekiel's tragic silence as a poet 'what to say or tell and what not to say' is in itself an agonizing situation. So quite naturally we take upon ourselves the unnecessary credential of involving self-assumed authenticities in order to live our lives according to our own assumptions. We don't know how to live as simple, unobtrusive and unassuming natural creatures. Therefore, Ezekiel conclude his poem *The Neutral* with the following words:

> *Yoga, Zen, Kabbala,*
> *St. John of the Cross, Pelmanism,*
> *Plotinus, Sell Your Way to Success,*
> *Kierkegaard, Pascal,*
> *Think and Grow Rich,*
> *The Four Quartets,*
> *and How to Change*
> *Yourself in Ten Days.*[39]

Almost all the poems included in his *The Unfinished Man* strike a note of personal defeat and loss. Referring to *The Unfinished Man* David McCutchion rightly observes:

> *Almost all the poems in* ***The Unfinished Man*** *are mildly sardonic 'case histories' of failure.*[40]

The note of failure on the part of man does not refer to any personal failure of individual man as a progressive specie. On the other hand, it envisages a typical cultural situation which pushed down man from his heights on human dignity. Precisely the failure is due to the demographic alterations because of the people preferring to settle in the cities. It is the city life that gets exposed. Man is the protagonist who really suffers in this demographic alterations. In a way humanity always aspires to achieve more and more intellectual heights of existence from time to time. The emergence of city in the cultural advancement process is in itself a defeatist erruption.

Man Fated to Unfinishedness

The very title *The Unfinished Man* maintains an ironic implication that man as a social and cultural product is on the sure way for his finish in being a dignified human. This is so because the finishing process is drastically advancing even though he is 'Unfinished' yet. The main reason for this emerging finishing process is to be found in man, being cut-off from nature, as well as from his own inherent human touch. The primal affections and aspirations of life, which are the most important symptoms of human, are recieving a terrible shock and disaster. In the very first poem such as disaster is complexly but humorously, presented as a painful reflection on the city dwellers agony of existence 'the hills are always far away' (Urban), 'at dawn he never sees the skies' (Urban). Even then 'the city like a passion burns' (Urban), the word 'burns' is used with the suggestive categorical pun implying that it burns the very human in him and not exactly awakening a burning passion. But, however, with all its inhuman dimensions, the city is a burning passion in the modern man.

The ironic critical appraisals of city life particulars on Ezekiel have their influence from the modern European poets like Baudelaire and T.S. Eliot. But, however, Ezekiel looks at this modern citizen of city with a sense of 'self-deprecatory uneasiness'.[41] His sympathy and concern for the type of fall in man of city is always there reflected in the tonal vibrations of the poems here. The pitiable state of the Urban man is reflected in the following lines:

The river which he claims be loves
Is dry, and all the winds lie dead.[42]

Again to quote:

The city like a passion burns
He dreams of morning walks, alone,
And floating on a wave of sand
But still his mind its traffic turns
Away from beach and tree and stone
To kindred clamour close at hand.[43]

It is because of this poetically vibrating tone of sympathy towards the fallenness of man, M. David observes 'Unlike Baudelaire, Mr. Ezekiel has considerable sympathy for his weak but well intentioned persona',[44] and Ezekiel is poetically nearer to T.S. Eliot in breeding in himself a sort of egotistically compassion towards the city dwellers. The most intriguing aspect of Ezekiel's poetry lies in the fact that he is himself a stern Bombay-wala, in spite of the fact that he nurtured in his poetic self all sorts of personal dream and visions of cosy and comfortable nearness to nature and verdure. But, however, the special distancing of city from the primeval pleasure of the sub-urban context is always a sort of haunting agony in the mind of a city dweller.

The tragic complexities of submitting oneself to the city life are obviously visible in the personal paralleling situations of experiencing the monotony of living in the city. Ezekiel is highly critical but not sneering. His attitude towards man fallenness has the echoes of W.H. Auden. He still maintains a sort of primal passion for poetry and imagination, which should ultimately elevate him from his unfortunate state of existence. The inevitable loss that he sustained in the city life and the unavoidable agony that agonises in the era thereof, must find a relief in poetry and poetic imagination. Therefore, Ezekiel prays:

Whatever the enigma,
The passion of the blood,
Grant me the metaphor
To make it human good.[45]

However, Ezekiel is consciously aware that such prayer have not great comfort in them in the city life. In his *Love Sonnet* the point becomes more clear. The lover says there in:

You and I wait for words;
our love has formed like dew
on summer nights.[46]

The 'dew' on 'summer nights' is an intriguing image. The dew never forms in the summer nights, even when it forms it evaporates the next moment because of the summer heat. So the life in which the lovers are staying, in spite of the fact that it 'Could house a passing cloud',[47] is not capable of providing for them a comfortable home. In an ultimate manner Ezekiel is of the conviction that: 'Home is where we have to gather grace'.[48] But, however, even the distant sea with all its 'A passionate and perpetual mystery',[49] could as well comfort the lovers:

We look in consort at the distant sea,
And fee! it turbulent and salty there,[50]

But this turbulence and saltiness is a welcome feature because of its inherent 'mystery' of primal nature. But the cafe is a hopeless place. Therefore, Ezekiel concludes his *Love Sonnet* in the most disasterous manner:

Floating down the hill, as on a cloud,
Proud as lovers are, inarticulate
We lose ourselves in mingling with the crowd,
Not unafraid of this ambiguous fate.
We look inquiringly at road and sky,
A certain happiness would be to die.[51]

The real poverty of the city life is in arriving at a conclusion that they are 'on a cloud', in spite of the fact that they are literally, 'floating down the hill'. Therefore, there is that inarticulate and ironically affecting pride as lovers. The only way to distinguish themselves from this stigmatic conditions is in mingling with the crowd. The crowd provides them the ananimity, if not needful privacy and comfort. Therefore, they put question marks on their faces and look at the 'road and the sky'. The road suggests the practical course of life in front of them and the sky suggests their unending aspirations of life. So in this context the certainity of happiness is in death only and not in a moment before. The *Love Sonnet* is neither a sonnet nor is it about love in its true sense. It is a mere blurt sound. (Etymologically sonnet means a small sound), emerging out of the broken heart of the love, i.e. the poet. *The Unfinished Man* is really document in vocally articulating the agony of being in the world in our times, where in we are totally denied of what our ancestors used to call 'happiness'. This loss is absolute, total, and unamendable, therefore, Ezekiel's man is near at hand for a total finish in being a city dweller. He is *The Unfinished Man,* yet, but Ezekiel's poetic prophecy is a writing on the wall. The whole humanity is surging with an evidity towards a finish. Such is the ironic intention suggested in the title *The Unfinished Man.*

The title of the collection *The Unfinished Man* is taken from W.B. Yeats. It goes without saying that Yeats suffered in himself a lot because of the boachedness of culture in our times. The lack of credentials of values so sickened W.B. Yeats to such an extend that he started denouncing everything including education. 'Prayer for my Daughter' is a standing testimony of Yeats' frustration. This is more or less true about Nissim Ezekiel also. In this context the words of Anisur Rahman are worth quoting:

> *The epigraph from Yeat's in* ***The Unfinished Man*** *explains, to a large extent, the position of the poet who has been brought face to face with his own clumsiness.*[52]

Clumsiness in City Life

The above reference to 'his own clumsiness' is a matter of vigorous self-search on the part of Ezekiel. The very first poem *Urban* characterizes the type of agony and clumsiness that the poet suffered in the context of the modern city life. Once again the lines of 'Urban' are worth quoting:

> *The city like a passion burns.*
> *He dreams of morning walks, alone,*
> *And floating on a wave of sand.*
> *But still his mind its traffic turns*

Away from beach and tree and stone
To kindred clamour close at hand.[53]

The reference to the distance sort by city 'from beach, tree and stone', is in itself an indication that the poet of city is not at home with himself in being a city dweller. The 'kindred clamour' close at hand sufficiently says about the disgusting noise pollution of the city life. All the poems in this volume, as characterized by Adil Jussawala are the 'records of the moral aches and pains of a modern Indian in one of his own cities'.[54] But, however, the so-called 'moral aches and pains' are made with a typical skeptical spirit of an individual, who ultimately terminates everything into a sort of humorous preposition, followed by a typical sense of criticism coupled with objectivity. Rajeev Taranath and Meena Belliappa in their '*Poetry of Nissim Ezekiel*' rightly point out the abundance of skepticism in Ezekiel:

> *Skepticism of various kinds, a very astringent*
> *kind of humour, a sharpness of expression*
> *reflecting back to the difficulty of*
> *discrimination*
> *all these are the consequent responses to the*
> *comparatively new and complex stimuli of the*
> *human milieu.*[55]

Finally the poems themselves become interesting because of their 'astringent kind of humour' and 'a sharpness of expression reflecting back to the difficulty of discrimination'. The 'complex stimuli of the human milieu', ultimately helps him to discover his own self and its contingent difficulties of adjusting with the world of existence. If so the existential agony provides a 'reference to the poetic self and the cultural milieu which has shaped it'.[56]

The ultimate burden of the poet reflects a grievance at the 'cultural milieu' which has shaped his poetic self. Most of the studies of Ezekiel have not taken this shattered poetic self into a serious considerations. It is his emotional involvement with the scenes of description that becomes really important. Ezekiel breeds in himself a typical suffering self which has no hope of relief. Because of the pathetic condition of the self of the poet, he is not in a position of any possible solution for the unfortunate state of human existence in our times. It is out of utter disgust that he masses modern man as *the unfinished man,* but surely and certainly on the road for the ultimate finish. Therefore, S. Sreenivasan rightly points out as follows:

> *There is an identification of the self with the scene, but it is not a self which analyzes and reflects or possesses a vision of an alternative social order or stage of things. At any rate, such a dynamic vision is not revealed in the poetry itself. The images of sordidness and deprivation evoke in the poet a mood of tiredness, self-pity and devotion, rather than protest or revolt.*[57]

Nissim Ezekiel in his poem *Something to Pursue* says as follows:

> *To save myself*
> *From what the city had made of me, I returned*
> *As intended to the city I had Known,*
> *Pity for myself suggested this*
> *And pity for the world.*[58]

Sreenivasan's contention that 'there is no protest or revolt in the poetry of Ezekiel' is not right. Every poem substantially characterizes the self of the poet as a protesting and revolting one. But, however, his incapacity to process 'a vision of alternative social order or state of things' need not be taken as lacking in positive dream or vision for the urban society.

Sense and Sensibility

What all Ezekiel wanted to suggests to the urban masses concerns with his harsh evocations to keep the sense and sensibility totally harmonized. If this harmony of senses and sensibilities is achieved it is just possible that life would not become a painful phenomena. It is his pity for the world that ultimately brings him to city that he had known 'I returned as intended to the city that I had known'. This he had done to save himself from 'what the city had made him'. The city of his choice is nothing but a city where all the people maintain a sort of harmony between their sense and sensibility. Therefore, says Ezekiel:

> *We were not made for love alone, my Love,*
> *Although our flesh and bones would have it so,*
> *A thousand small intricacies of brain*
> *Hold my blood-streams captive, which will not flow*
> *Freely to serve the ends of love, until*
> *They know the various ways of men,*
> *The soul in solitude and God revealed.*[59]

Reference to 'a thousand small intricacies of brain' holding 'blood stream captive' suggests at the true love that he cherishes. It is with this true love that he can find his 'soul in solitude and God revealed'. A romantically idealized world would not do for him. According to him there is an urgent need for man to explore the possibility of living in harmony with himself. If such harmony is achieved the agonies of city, are for that matter the agonies of being in the world of existence are not going to be problems. Therefore, until and unless such harmony is achieved man is likely to remain really unfinished.

Two Poetic Themes

Quite naturally, his poetic themes are divided into two clear-cut dimensions. One group represents the subjective personal experiences of a poet whose intimate perspectives are in the form of a flux where with the objective representation becomes a typical suggestive symbol of his felt experiences. These experiences of Ezekiel are significantly humorous in this sense that they aspire for a consistent calm and quiet attitude of life in a world stuffed with confusions. In this context his highest poetic purpose is at once humanistic in aspiration and an intimate involvement into the world around him. The other theme of his poetry concerns with an objective poetic achievement based upon ironic observations of the world of the people around him. It is here that a sort of paradoxical formulation of the characters of the people. This paradoxical formula emerges out of the human hypocrisis counter painted by the formulized ways of existence of the people. The people around him appear to be a lost generation who do not have any clear ideas of decent life.

In *Three Women* Ezekiel refers to the kind of people who are completely satisfied with the basic instinctively satisfaction of life:

They spoke the language
of food and love
naturally
as a mother-tongue;
no problem here
of accent or of intonation.[60]

This complacent world of the people, is essentially a vulgar; and this vulgarity is entrenched in the modern civilization. 'Bosched civilization' gives him an agonizing opportunity to make the themes of his satirical poems. Therefore, immediately following the above lines Ezekiel submits its concern for the world as follows:

The simplicity,
the directness,
the elation
of the food-love offered
serve as a norm
for all my life's
daily hell or heaven
improvised, missing
or attaining form.[61]

'The simplicity, the directness, the elation' of the 'food-love' complacency of the world arrests his sense of decency but his is the norm of the world. For a 'lifetime it serves as a daily hell or heaven'. For the poet himself this kind of instinctive limitations of the people is a hell itself. But, for the people around him it is just 'a heaven improvized, missing or attaining form'. Therefore, in his poem *Transparently*
Ezekiel makes the following remarks:

It's fantasitc
what a slave
a man can be
who has nobody
to oppress him
except himself.[62]

It is evident from above that man himself is ultimate maker of fate and nemesies by way of resorting to the instinctive needs as though they are self-sufficient. But, for Ezekiel him self this kind of life offers no, happiness at all. Therefore, he says:

And don't tell me
there's any happiness
in being compulsive
or mindless.[63]

It is evident that the needlessness of the world is for him 'a falling of a most terrible thing'. He wants to take up for himself a definite task of capturing it in all his poetry and preserving it for the reading public as a point of serious concern. Therefore, says Ezekiel:

Who wants experience
at the cost of achievement?

All I want now
is the recognition
of dilemma
and the quickest means
of resolving it
within my limits.[64]

Lakshmi Raghunandan pertinently remarks about Ezekiel

in his essay on "Nissim Ezekiel" that:

> *Thematically, his poems range from the purely subjective mystical experiences of a psyche afloat on a flusionary circumanbience as in 'Two Images', through the intensely sensual enjoyment of the physical intimacy between man and woman as in 'Nudes', to an objective often ironic observation of extrasensory paradoxical events resulting as much from human hypocrisy as from the very nature of life itself.*[65]

For this purpose he invents his metaphors to re-enact his own experiences into poetry. In his poems, we find the features of expressionism, loconic juxtapositions and social problems taken up for a symbolist impressionistic re-structuring of experiences. His obstractions are very often concretely contextualized in sustained metaphors. Probably in the whole of Anglo-Indian poetry of our times Ezekiel alone encompasses wide canvas of enveloping the entire external world by way of finding a potential metaphoric consistency. Therefore, the remarks of L. Raghunandan are very important here:

> *A Christian terminology to express concern with the inner life, an optimistic expectation of the evolution of a new man, and autotelic metaphors to re-enact an inner experience are some of the features of Expressionism existant in Ezekiel's poetry, but polychromatically juxtaposed with sexual themes and social problems to generate a symbolist impressionist proclivity restructuring an experience; 'to improvise my later fiction', as Ezekiel himself remarks, and contextualize abstractions in sustained metaphors.*[66]

Nissim Ezekiel's central aim in poetry appears to be representing India in all its entirety of the present-day operation. In spite, of the fact that the Indian situation is very unfortunate and low in being a humanistic civilization, Ezekiel felt a sort of personal intimacy and fondness for this Indian situation. As a citizen of India he felt proud of his motherland. He maintained a sort of love-hate-tangle-relationship with the modern India. This aspect of Ezekiel will be taken in the next chapter.

REFERENCES

1. P. P. Mehta, 'Nissim Ezekiel', *Contemporary Indo-English Verse (A Collection* of *Critical Essays on Male Poets)*, Vol. II, ed. N.A. Dwivedi (Bareilly: Prakash Book Depot, 1984), p. 211.
2. Nissim Ezekiel, *Latter-Day Psalms* (Delhi: Oxford University Press, 1982), p. 59.
3. Michael Roberts, ed., *The Fabers Book* of *Modern Verse* (London: Faber and Faber Ltd., 1965), p. 104.
4. *Ibid.*, p. 61.
5. P. Lal, 'An Arrival in Indo-Anglian Poetry', *The Alien Insiders: Essays on Indian Writing in English* (Calcutta: A Writers Workshop Book, 1987), p. 85.
6. Quotation taken from the Unpublished thesis of Dr. S. B. K. Murthy, *Wallace Stevens and Existentialism* (Raipur: Pt. avishankar University, 1979), p. 20.
7. P. Lal, 'An Arrival in Indo-Anglian Poetry', *The Alien Insiders: Essays on Indian Writing in English* (Calcutta: A Writers Workshop Book, 1987), p. 86.
8. Inder Nath Kher, ed., *Journal of South Asian Literature,* Vol. XI, Nos. 3-4 (Spring, Summer 1976), p. 17.
9. Quotation taken from the unpublished thesis of Dr. S.B.K. Murthy, *Wallace Stevens and Existentialism* (Raipur: Pt. Ravishankar University, 1979), p. 20.
10. Inder Nath Kher, ed., *Journal of South Asian Literature,* Vol. XI, Nos. 3-4 (Spring, Summer 1976), p. 17.

11. P. Lal, 'An Arrival in Indo-Anglian Poetry', *The Alien Insiders: Essays on Indian Writing in English* (Calcutta: A Writers Workshops Book, 1987), p. 86.
12. *Ibid.*, p. 87.
13. *Ibid.*,
14. Inder Nath Kher, ed., *Journal* of *South Asian Literature*, Vol. XI, Nos. 3-4 (Spring Summer 1976), p. 13.
15. P.S. Kasture, 'The Nature of Chaos in Modern Indo-Anglian Poetry', *Recent Commonwealth Literature* Vol. II, ed. R.K. Dhawan, P.V. Dhamija, AK. Shrivastava (New Delhi: Prestige Book, 1989), p. 56.
16. P. Lal, 'An Arrival in Indo-Anglian Poetry', *The Alien Insiders: Essays on Indian Writing in English* (Calcutta: A Writers Workshop Book, 1987), p. 89.
17. P. Lal, 'An Arrival in Indo-Anglian Poetry', *The Alien Insiders: Essays on Indian Writing in English* (Calcutta: A Writers Workshop Book, 1987), p. 90.
18. Inder Nath Kher, ed., *Journal* of *South Asian Literature*, Vol. XI, Nos. 3-4 (Spring, Summer 1976), p. 12.
19. P.P. Mehta, 'Nissim Ezekiel', *Contemporary Indo-English Verse* Vol. II (A *Collection* of *Critical Essays on Male Poets)*, ed. A.N. Dwivedi (Bareilly : Prakash Book Depot, 1984), p. 211.
20. Nissim Ezekiel, *Latter-Day Psalms* (Delhi: Oxford University Press, 1982), p. 14
21. P.P. Mehta, 'Nissim Ezekiel', *Contemporary Indo-English Verse Vol. II (A Collection of Critical Essays on Male Poets)*, ed. A.N. Dwivedi (Bareilly : Prakesh Book Depot, 1984), p. 212.
22. *Ibid.*,
23. *Ibid.*,
24. *Ibid.*, p. 213.
25. *Ibid.*,
26. Cleanth Brooks and R.P. Warren, *Understanding Poetry* (New York : Hart and Winston, 1938), p. 6.
27. *Ibid.*, p. 6.
28. Nissim Ezekiel, 'Ideas and Modern Poetry', (Indian Writers in Conference, 1964), pp. 48-54.
29. S.N. Prasad, 'The Cognitive Self in Nissim Ezekiel: An

Approach to His Poetry', *Indian English Literature: Since Independence,* ed. A. K. Panikar. (New Delhi: The Indian Association for English Studies, 1991), p. 124.

30. *Ibid.,* p. 125.
31. Nissim Ezekiel, *Latter-Day Pslams* (Delhi: Oxford University Press, 1982), p. 53.
32. D.J. Enright and E.D. Chickera, *English Critical Texts: 16th Century to 20th Century* (London: Oxford University Press, 1968), p. 191.
33. Nissim Ezekiel, *Latter-Day Psalms* (Delhi : Oxford University Press, 1982), p. 50.
34. Christopher Wiseman, 'The Development of Technique in the Poetry of Nissim Ezekiel: From Formality to Informality', *Considerations.* ed. M. Mukherjee (New Delhi: Allied Publishers. Pvt. Ltd., 1977), p. 144.
35. Inder Nath Kher, ed., *Journal of South Asian Literature,* Vol. XI, Nos. 3-4 (Spring, Summer 1976), p. 129.
36. *Ibid.*
37. Michael Robert, ed., *Faber Book of Modern Verse* (London: Faber and Faber, 1965), p. 91.
38. Inder Nath Kher, ed., *Journal of South Asian Literature,* Vol. XI, Nos. 3-4 (Spring, Summer 1976), p. 129.
39. *Ibid.,* p. 130.
40. David McCutchion, 'Examen De Midi', *Indian Writing in English* (Calcutta: Writers Workshop, 1969), p. 119.
41. *Ibid.,* p. 120.
42. Nissim Ezekiel, *Latter-Day Psalms* (Delhi : Oxford University Press, 1982), p. 58.
43. *Ibid.*
44. David McCutchion, 'Examen De Midi:, *Indian Writing in English* (Calcutta: Writers Workshop, 1969), p. 120.
45. Nissim Ezekiel, *Latter-Day Pslams* (Delhi : Oxford University Press, 1982), p. 59.
46. Inder Nath Kher, ed., *Journal of South Asian Literature,* Vol. XI, Nos. 3-4, (Spring, Summer 1976), p. 64.
47. *Ibid.*

48. Nissim Ezekiel, *Latter-Day Psalms* (Delhi : Oxford University Press, 1982), p. 59.
49. Inder Nath Kher, ed., *Journal of South Asian Literature,* Vol. XI, Nos. 3-4 (Spring, Summer 1976), p. 64.
50. *Ibid.*
51. *Ibid.*
52. Anisur Rahman, *Form and Value in the Poetry of Nissim Ezekiel* (New Delhi: Abhinav Publication, 1981), p. 36.
53. Inder Nath Kher, ed., *Journal of South Asian Literature,* Vol. XI, Nos. 3-4 (Spring, Summer 1976), p. 58.
54. Anisur Rahman, *Form and Value in the Poetry of Nissim Ezekiel* (New Delhi: Abhinav Publication, 1981), p. 36.
55. Rajeev Taranath and Meena Belliappa, *The Poetry of Nissim Ezekiel* (Calcutta: A Writers Workshop, 1966), p. 64.
56. S. Sreenivasan, 'The Self and its Enchanted Circle: A Perspective on the Poetry of Nissim Ezekiel', *Changing Traditions in Indian English Literature,* P.K. Rajan, ed. (New Delhi: Creative Books, 1995), p. 151.
57. *Ibid.,* pp. 152-53.
58. *Ibid.*
59. Inder Nath Kher, ed., *Journal of South Asian Literature,* Vol. XI, Nos. 3-4 (Spring Summer 1976), p. 20.
60. *Ibid.,* p. 89.
61. *Ibid.*
62. *Ibid.,* p. 87.
63. *Ibid.*
64. *Ibid.,* p. 88.
65. Lakshmi Raghunandan, 'Nissim Ezekiel', *Contemporary Indian Poetry of English* (New Delhi: Reliance Publishing House, 1990), p. 11.
66. *Ibid.*

5
The Voice of India

Nissim Ezekiel is a typical modern Indo-Anglian poet for whom India is his Motherland. In spite of the fact that he comes of a Jewish parentage, and Jews being the ancient most migrants to India, his emotional attachment to India and the manner in which he celebrates his Indianism in his poetry is in itself a matter of intense devotion towards the country as a whole. That way Ezekiel is a modern poet with a sort of skeptical attitude towards the emotional factors in life, including love. But, however, there are innumerable poems of him which go to celebrate India in innumerable ways. Depending upon his mood sometimes he is devotional as in *In India,* sometimes he is intensely passionate about its ancestory and tradition *Background Casually,* yet sometimes he is critical of its age worn traditions, faiths, and beliefs as *Night of the Scorpion.* In an over all manner he expresses a typical disgust at the backwardness and at the unfeeling nature of Indian polity as a close knit society. India is a land of innumerable cultures, traditions, religions. Therefore, for an objective observation the lifestyles in India offer incongruities in themselves; and, thereby, presenting India as a land of immensely laughable dimensions. As a poet Ezekiel involve himself with India and its Indianism in such a critical manner that it all becomes a profound satire on the back looking Indians and their orthodox traditions and operations.

But at the same time, his crisp love for India and his passionate devotion it as his Motherland confer upon him a rare distinction of a poet who considers India as a home-land and celebrated it in divine sublimities. Nissim Ezekiel looks at India with the peculiar temperaments of a disillusioned person. He was born and brought up in Bombay. But, he has many inhuman things to tell about Bombay as a city. This kind of skeptical and hopeless manner of looking at Bombay is born of his greater thematic concern which he borrowed from Baudelaire, T.S. Eliot, W.H. Auden and the like European poets. They all looked upon city as a boneless, inhuman uglification of people, whose human touch is almost nil. In a city there is no positive human culture. There is only a way of life which conforms its people into the so-called capsulized vocations which do not have anything to do with human temperaments and human intentionalities at large. But, Ezekiel's grasp of the total Indian rhythmic movements of life is simple and asounding. Referring to Ezekiel's Indianism. P.P. Mehta has to say as follows:

> *We find a typical type of Indian atmosphere in the poems of Ezekiel. The Indian society, the Indian relationship between society and nature surprise the reader with their freshness of approach and observation.*[1]

The 'freshness of approach and observation' emerges out of his ironical detachment; and he enjoys his own detachment in the manner of serious thinker, as Ezekiel himself says:

> *Scores of my poems, are obviously written for personal, therapeutic purposes.*[2]

The 'personal, therapeutic purposes', that he refers here concerns with the exhausting and choice manner of looking at the Indian people's ignorance. their backwardness, and their innocence, and not the least, their vain and purposeless manner of existence.

His Love of India

Ezekiel's love for India and its people is a certain poetic fact in his heart. Also the manner in which he wishes to introduce a sense of reformation in its people is equally important. Precisely speaking, Ezekiel wanted a sort of total revolution and reformation in the unmeaning orthodox traditions, fates and beliefs of the people. The manner in which he looks at them with a serious introspection warrants a self-discovery for the poet himself. The introspective detachment with all its humorous and ironic turns and movements ultimately brings into him a sort of 'therapeutic' relief. Towards the end of the *Night of the Scorpion,* the poet has to say as follows:

> *I watched the flame feeding on my mother.*
> *I watched the holy man perform his rites*
> *to tame the poison with an incantation.*
> *After twenty hours*
> *it lost its sting.*[3]

In spite of all the humour and irony at the expense of the others, there is a typical involvement into a situation itself in *Night of the Scorpion.* He was simply moved by the harrowing pain that his mother had undergone. In stating 'I watched the flame feeding on my mother', the poet himself sympathetically under goes the 'feeding flame' in himself. This is particularly the holistic manner in which Ezekiel characterizes himself as a concerned and emotionalized observer of the situation. His, irony, his satire, and his disgust at the Indian ways of life is something that is born of his intense feeling of affectionate sympathy towards Indian life.

Expressing his typical passionate love for India, Ezekiel says as follows in his *Naipaul's India and Mine*:

> *India is simply my environment. A man can do some thing for and in his enviornment by being fully what he is, by not withdrawing from it. I have not withdrawn from India.*[4]

To some extent it is his child-like interest for observing things in a typical contrary manner, particularly when forbidden to do so. A child is often tempted to do something which is forbidden. Frank Birbal Singh in his interview with Nissim Ezekiel asked a very important question which goes as follows:

> Q. *Did you at any stage take an interest in Indian philosophy or religion?*[5]

Ezekiel's answer for the above question is in one-way revelation of his contrary temper or temperament in being an observer of men and matters around him. Ezekiel's answer goes as follows:

> *A. Oh, certainly. That started for me at a very early age. I was, after all in a Roman Catholic school, and the Fathers used to say to the students that there was nothing at all in Hinduism. The Hindus, Parsees, Moslems, all said, 'What? There is nothing in Hinduism?' So we started reading the* Gita *and Upanishads at school, which I may not have done in the next ten years, had the Fathers not said there was nothing in it. I have always felt that substanttial truths about life are expressed in Hinduism, Islam, Judaism, Christianity.*[6]

Ezekiel gives a great emotional importance for all the important religions of the world including Hinduism. In spite of the fact that his attraction for Hinduism as a certain emotional fact of his life, he never became dogmatic or encircle himself in blind faiths. On the contrary, in accordance with his skeptical temper he raises very pertinent doubts concerning the Indian ways of life. He ever goes to the extent of satirizing and harshly laughing at the ignorant and innocent masses of India. But, however, he does not really aim at stinging or causing pain to the objects of his satire in being satirical, he adopts for himself a typical sense of irony. Paniker K. Ayyappa in his *Beyond Irony: The Third Vision of Nissim Ezekiel* rightly points out as follows:

> *Two kinds of irony seem to operate in the poetry of Nissim Ezekiel: one closely allied to satire, where the poet stands at a distance from the object looked at; the other, closely allied to compassion, where the poet examines the experience as if from within.*

> *Examples of the first kind are more numerous among his early writing; they are less common in the later period.*
> *In the middle poems, the two kinds appear to co-exist. The direction of the poet's development is therefore clear: exceptions might be there, only to confirm the main line of development.*[7]

His Jewish descent on the one hand, and his natural adaptation to the Hindu culture on the other hand, made him a tolerant and sympathetic observer of life and life-styles in India. William Walsh has something very interesting to point out about Ezekiel and his concern for India. Says W. Walsh as follows:

> *If Ezekiel has on one side the inhibiting discontinuity of a gap between himself and the living, used language, he has on another side a second but very different, creative discontinuity. This is constituted by his being of Jewish descent in a Hindu culture. It is both a theme of his poetry and a source of considerable energy in it..........................*
>
> *Nissim Ezekiel in the Indian scene is a permanent expatriate, but one who has freely elected to stay. Displaced by his own spiritual past, he is in place by an act of the will. His eye is familiar with, but at a distance from, the object, and his specifically Indian poetry is both inward and detached, a combination making for a peculiar strength and validity.*[8]

Ezekiel accepted India as his home and his own place, 'by an act of the will'; but, at the same time, the objectivity that he acquires for himself confers a distinction of dilettante and humorous stance upon him. There are innumerable poems in which he lashes at India and the Indian situations. But, in all of them there is a sympathy of an earnest lover of the culture. The poems like *Background Casually, Island, In India, Enterprise, Central, Healers, Cows, Yeshwant Jagtap, Very Indian Poems in Indian English, Night of the Scorpion,* Ezekiel expresses his typical love-tangle with his Indian context. In his *Background Casually,* he says:

I have made my commitments now
This is one to stay where I am,
As others choose to give themselves.
In some remote and backward place.
My backward place is where I am.[9]

The ironic manner in which he turns against himself, when he says 'My backward place is where I am', is in itself an indication that he poetically characterizes the Indian situation with the sympathetic eye of the insider, where his commitments are genuine to the culture he adopts. The very first title poem of his *A Time to Change* is implicatively reminiscent of his concerns to come back to his own house i.e. India. The poem *A Time to Change* starts with a question:

We who leave the house in April, Lord,
How shall we return?[10]

The above lines reflects at Ezekiel's humbleness and humility in acknowledging the possible corruptions that spoiled his temperament, particularly when he was in London. Ezekiel in London must have been corrupted by 'unlawful desires' and 'strange Gods'. He considers himself to have been defiled by foreign practices. Quite naturally the theme of the poem concerns with torments of his mind which make him restless and which hasten him towards discipline, purpose, order and stability. Therefore, his prime concerns all through his life are mainly manners of projecting himself bravely and uninhibitedly, loving his fellowmen and family, and a proper conduct and discipline which can be redeemed:

> *In the private country of my mind*
> *Where the worser part, as Socrates would say,*
> *Presides.*[11]

So with this kind of passion and love for India, Ezekiel approaches the Indian theme.

His Major Themes

The continuing themes of Ezekiel are always life in the city, sexuality, the problems of marriage and the need to overcome the same, alienation, the desire to belong, and a keen intention to create an integration for himself among the various discordant and contrary aspects of his character and temperament. All these things are intensely reflected in his poems on Indian life.

It may be seen that in the thematic properties of the above there is nothing particularly or peculiarly Indian except the atmosphere. In a way the themes are universal; and it is perinially interesting to note how Ezekiel conforms them to the Indian situations and circumstances, culturally speaking. The Indian circumstances particularly become important because of the widespread ignorance of the people; and illiteracy being a definite phenomena is India (80per sent of the people are illiterate), helplessness and a certain amount of cynicism and pessimism become highly contextual. Innocence on the one hand and dogmatic traditionalism on the other hand conforms India to a sort of resigned manner of living lives as mere vegetables, rather than as spirited individualistic human agents.

The fundamental cause of ignorance in Indian masses emerges out of the irrational metaphysical faiths (or fears) which completely smash out the rational counters of imaginations. As a matter of fact the Indians have never resented to the state of understanding nature and fellowmen in an empirical manner, which prompts the fundamental theory of cause and effect phenomena of nature. A typical Indian still believes that all the causes of material effects in the world are to be found in the metaphysical mysterious forces of heaven. An average Indian considers the practical world as illusory; and he conforms his thoughts and action to the typical manner of ignorantly perceiving the words within the ambit of his unfounded faiths and undependable deductions. At the outset, Ezekiel in his poetry, is typically concerned with the idea of absolutely rationalizing the attitudes of the Indian masses. According to him this rationalization on Indian thought and action is possible with the help of poetry. Therefore, his poetry concerns itself with the idea of delicately presenting the incongruities of the lives of the people around him. Needless to say that the manner in which Ezekiel presents this incongruities is ironic and humorous.

Their decisions and manner in which they prefer to live their lives are in themselves incongruous; and therefore, they are contigently humorous. Abject poverty on one hand, and ignorance on the other, force them to live on an as-is-where-is-basis, without any positive aspirations and achievements. Therefore, Ezekiel looks at the Indian scenario with a sort of skepticism and disgust. Unlike V.S. Naipaul or Salman Rushdi who look at India with a great hatred, Ezekiel conforms himself to the art of sympathetically evoking a sense of pity towards the Indian situation. But, to the extend that he loves India as his own motherland, his sympathies and dispositions are highly appreciable. Even at the point of repetition the words of Lakshmi Raghunandan are worth quoting here. Nissim Ezekiel's poems according to her approach as:

> *. . . to an objective often ironic observation of extrasensory paradoxical events resulting as much from human hypocrisy as from the very nature of life itself.*[12]

While a certain amount of human hypocrisy, is a definite fact about the Indians 'the paradoxical events' need not necessarily be extra sensory as such. Depending upon the situations, the behavioural patterns of the Indian masses take interesting turns and movements.

The Force of Superstitions

Nissim Ezekiel's poem *Night of the Scorpion* is a very interesting poem which presents the popular superstition of the Indian masses. As a matter of fact, there is no rational manner of understanding or withstanding the problem here R. Taranath and M. Belliappa characterized the poem as:

> *The observer's neutral attitude to the scene, balancing the supertitious with the presence of the father, 'sceptic, rationalist', makes the supernatural a poetically credible quantity in an episode which stands transformed into an experience of significance, at least to the believers.*[13]

Scorpions stinging the people is a very common phenomena in the suburban areas of India. Scorpion is a tropical pest; and the pain of its sting is in itself quite unbearable physically as well as mentally. In the context of protagonises child-like emotional agitations and anxieties are understandable. But, in the presence of the superstitions of advisors, which the poem the mother in the family was stung by a scorpion. Quite naturally she is restless and suffers from acute pain. Out of this situation Ezekiel humorously brings out a typical ironic manner of the attending agents in treating the patient. This poem can be taken as one of the finest example of black humour. Instead of going for some sort of rationally approved pain killer, all the relatives and the attending neighbours resort to all sorts of superstitions and propositions of curing. In fact, it is the mother of the protagonist that received the sting. To that extent the includes his rationalist father also, he becomes a mere mute observer trying to contain the pain of his mother silently and sympathetically in himself. But, the protagonist is conscious of the absurdity ruling the roost in the situation. There is a tendency among Indians to consider any sort of pain as a metaphysical formula of reminding people about the needful other-worldly philosophy of life they must ultimately evolve for themselves. Pain, according to the back looking Indian philosophy should become a sort of reminder for the people in order to make them resigned from the desires in this life. Also they believe that it is through pain only that man becomes purified. Hence:

> *The peasants came like swarms of flies and buzzed the Name of God a hundred times to paralyse the Evil One.*[14]

This is the height of their superstition and unwithstandable at that in taking the 'Name of God' hundred times to ward off the 'Evil One'. One has a significant reference to Christian metaphor throughout also. The repercussion of the fight between God and Satan in the Christian mythology targeting man as the sufferer in itself is an absurd metaphysics. Indians are also equally God-fearing. It is this sense of God-fear that makes them conscious for themselves a typical altruistic philosophy of life. Indians particularly believe in reincarnation. Therefore, they tried to console the patient:

> *May the sins of your previous birth be burned*
> *away tonight, they said.*
> *May your suffering decrease the misfortunes of*
> *your next birth, they said.*
> *May the sum of evil balanced in this unreal world*
> *against the sum of good become diminished by*
> *your pain.*[15]

From the practical scorpion the streak of imagination transcending to innumerable births and deaths is in itself ridiculous and absurd. But nobody can help it. Such is the extend of poverty of imagination. In pronouncing:

May the poison purify your flesh
of desire, and your spirit of ambition.
they said, and they sat around
on the floor with my mother in the centre,
the peace of understanding on each face.[16]

The poet is the only person who is emotionally concerned in watching 'the flame feeding on my mother'. Ultimately the holy men tried to 'tame the poison with an incarnation'. We have here all the paraffinoid of mystic cures and metaphysical advices. It is very difficult to know whether the father's act of 'putting a match' to the bitten toe aggravated the pain or lessened it. In spite of the fact that he is a rationalist his act in the present context definitely contributed for more pain being added to the already unbearable pain of the mother. Quite naturally:

After twenty hours
it lost its stings.[17]

The poem expressionistically presents innumerable vollies of structural strokes. But the end stroke is quite interesting and humorous:

My mother only said
Thank God the scorpion picked on me and
spared my children.[18]

Innumerable critics pointed out that the sting itself is "a symbol of evil".[19] This concept of reading evil in the context makes a holistic stride towards apprehending the aesthetics of evil, in the Christian context. There is a way of reading this poem as a ridiculous parody of the 'Book of Job' in the *Holy Bible*. M.K. Naik in his article on Ezekiel 'The Tale is in the Sting' says that:

> *It would, therefore, be more appropriate to characterize the basic theme of the poem as the mystery of Evil and the enigma of the suffering attendant upon it.*[20]

The biblical analogy here is quite casual and non-serious. Therefore, it is a light-hearted parody. The mystery of evil and enigma of suffering attended upon it are in themselves suggestive of the metaphysical dimensions reached by Ezekiel in quite a humorous manner. It is just possible that he is trying to laugh at the absurd conceptual formulas of evils both in the Christainity and in the Eastern religions. Christopher Wiseman in his essay 'The Development of Technique in the Poetry of Nissim Ezekiel' rightly pointed out that:

> ***'Night of the Scorpion'*** *remains an interesting and very valid poem, containing a fascinating tension between personal crisis and mocking social observation,. . .* [21]

Suspension of Sense and Sensibility

Psychologically speaking there are two levels of human psyche where decisions are taken: Emotional plane and Rational plane. Whenever, any decision is taken at an emotional plane, duly prompted by the personal crisis, the decision itself is likely to be a phenomena of distancing from reason. In his essay on 'Metaphysical Poets' T.S. Eliot substantially pointed out at the 'dissociation of sensibility', which onset on humanity some time in the sixteenth century. This dissociation concerns with the cleavage between sense and sensibility. T.S. Eliot finds a cleavage between sense and sensibility in almost all the generations that emerged after the sixteenth century. Philosophically speaking this is what generally called as Cartesian Dichotomy, after the name of its progenitor Des Cartes.

It is ingenious on the part of Ezekiel to invent a poetic situation capable of observing Eliot's dissociation of sensibility syndrome and Cartesian cleavage. According to the strict rationalistic credentials it is not really possible to arrive at any right decision in a movement of personal emotional crisis. From this angle it is easy to understand Ezekiel's point of view. Life's decisions are such that they are bound, to be absurd in so far as they culminate from the emotional state. This is what Sigmund Freud envisaged. In the human set there is no real possibility of totally distancing the emotional plane and seeking total objectivity in making decisions. This is so because of the fact that the human personal sensibility is always a typical urgency to arrive at some decisions or the other. In all the moments of life, since the emotional plane is a definite circumstantial agent in deriving man to make his decision, right decision never come forward. This is the ultimate message of Ezekiel. The unfortunate human situation in the Indian context suited his poetic and philosophical purposes well. As he himself says he 'projects his poems from his own backward situation with the prime purpose of suggesting at the abundant sound and fury of the human activities'. The Indian situation in his poems is a mere occasional and situational property in arriving at his own poetic images. Otherwise his concern are with the whole humanity which always rushes in arriving at right decisions. This is the ultimate skeptical stance of Ezekiel as a poet of humanity.

From the point of view of providing cultural discomforts in India. Ezekiel's *Background Casually* is very important. Being a land of many religions he categorically brings the dominating and humiliating atmosphere in the schools created by the boys belonging to different cults and creeds. Even young children attending a Roman Catholic schools are not tolerant to the students belonging to other religions. He characterizes himself as:

The Frightened child who would not eat
Or sleep, a boy of meagre bone,[22]

The poem itself starts with a statement which objectively turns against the poet himself quite humorously in a very casual manner. Says Ezekiel:

'A poet-rascal-clown was born.'[23]

The clustered three designation, i.e. the poet-rascal-clown is in itself reflective of how, probably, his colleagues used to tease him. While the rascal and the clown are negative propositions, the poet is a complacent epithet that he claims for himself, with a little bit of felt pride in himself. He is a rascal and a clown because of the fact as for his own comprehension, he was quite a naughty and observant student, with the clownish slant of pulling the legs of everybody. What all he assumes about himself can be casually brushed off as a mere statement emerging out of infelt humiliation in the atmosphere in the school. The following lines violently present the most uncomfortable atmosphere in his school:

I went to Roman Catholic school,
A mugging Jew among the wolves.
They told me I had killed the Christ,
That year I won the scripture prize.
A Muslim sportsman boxed my ears.

I grew in terror of the strong
But undernourished Hindu lads,
Their prepositions always wrong,
Repelled me by passivity.
One noisy day I used a knife.[24]

In a Catholic School and he is a Jew. His Catholic friends who are characterized here as 'wolves', were in the habit of humiliating and hounding him because his Jewish ancestors were responsible for the crucifixion of Jesus Christ. Even in the Western world the Jews had to face this humiliating situation throughout the twentieth century. This kind of rational antagonism does not give a freedom of atmosphere, for particularly young students in their schools even in India. The Christian school antagonism is again coupled with the 'Muslim students' bullying manners and the 'Hindu students' helpless manner. In spite of the fact that they are in a majority the Hindu students are quite helpless because they are physically 'undernourished'. Even for his young brain the prepositions of these Hindu boys appear wrong. But, it is so because of their passivity. Therefore, the entire school atmosphere was awfully uncomfortable for the poet. He was so humiliated that on 'one noisy day' he went to the extend of using a knife, out of his psychological unrest. These two stanzas of *Background Casually* speak volumes about the uncongenial nature of school life in India. If this could be so in Bombay, there is no use of telling anything about the other places. In nutshell Ezekiel captured the uncongenial atmosphere created by the school-going child in India. We are usually proud of multi-racial, multi-lingual and multi-religious cluster of India. For that matter we have created a sublime praise of unity in diversity. It is all perfectly alright on a theor itical plane. But in the practical context our everyday reality envasages one simple unpleasant truth. We are incapable of co-existing as one human race. As a result in our personal encounters, as well as in our public life, we often find ourselves falling into unnecessary and in avoidable strives land fights. The plain truth is our national qualities of love, pity and sympathy are undermined by our surface social and cultural variations. This kind of inborn hatred on the basis of belonging to different religions and creeds is exactly the cultural problem that always undermines the human dignity of our nation. It is this point that Ezekiel substantially concretes in his *Background Casually*.

Love and Affection for his Motherland

In the 'Domestic front' there are all sorts of prayers and rituals. With this kind of descordant atmosphere 'his morals had declined'. It is quite a bold confessional statement. After considering many vocational prospects for himself imaginatively in India he left for England for his further studies. In England also there are three aspects with which he was required to contend. They are 'Philosophy, Poverty and Poetry', shared in a basement room. Even in England his life was not comfortable because of the innumerable violent incidents in the world. He started looking upon India with a sense of love. His home in India economically speaking was not an effluent one. His ancestors were forced to crushing seeds and producing oil for their sustenance. In spite of poverty and this kind of uncomfortable background it makes him look at his country again, presently with the sense of love and affection. Ezekiel had practically experienced in his life the hazards of living away from ones own motherland. After having faced many inner and outer storm he got the idea of coming back home, i.e. India, says Ezekiel:

The Indian landscape sears my eyes.
I have become a part of it
To be observed by foreigners.
They say that I am singular,
Their letters overstate the case.[25]

His foreign friends considered his desire to go back to India as a sign of his immaturity and backwardness. They called him 'singular' in being a fellow going from England to India. But, however, Ezekiel shares a passionate entanglement with India as his motherland. This feeling in him reigned supreme in heart al through his life. With all the defects, shortcomings and the disgusting social and cultural conditions, India becomes lovable for him. The concluding lines of the poem *Background Casually* are simply full of affection and love for India, says Ezekiel:

I have made my commitments now.
This is one: to stay where I am,
As others choose to give themselves
In some remote and backward place.
My backward place is where I am.[26]

The committed manner in which he expresses his love for India as his own homeland is a certain fact in his life.

Coming back to India, emotionally speaking, amounts to coming to the centre of his themes. Even if this centre is dubbed as backward place he simply does not bother about it. Even if it were to be really a backward place, he achieves his complete balance and harmony of being in the world. Homecoming is always a matter of a passionate and loveable experience. The background is definitely uncongenial. But, the manner in which he achieves for himself an emotional sense of harmony and balance matters most.

Images of Modern India

Nissim Ezekiel's concern for India are with the present in the sense that he considers modern India seriously in his poetry. Its traditional past with all its glories does not give him any great inspiration.

The cultural past of India, because of its religious differences, does not give him a fond personal love in experience. So far, as the past traditional aspects are concerned he was always critical, nay, even cynically ironic. In his poem *At Fifty* he is quite vocal about his resentment to the traditional past of India:

It is the tail now
that wags the dog.
Experience however real,
is, after all, over.
I do not want the ashes
of the old fire but the flame itself.
Interest in the secrets of renewal
is a sign of age,
no longer secret.[27]

In stating that 'the tail now that wags the dog', Ezekiel is indicating as to how the traditional past (i.e. the tail) controls the present. He does not invite for himself the 'old fire' he just wants the present 'flame itself'. He fervently believes for 'a renewal'; and given the choice he wants to identify himself with present-day India. In this context Ezekiel's conviction that he expressed in *Naipaul's India and Mine* is important:

> *I am not a Hindu and my background makes me*
> *a natural outsider: circumstances and decisions*
> *relate me to India. . .*
> *I cannot identify myself with India's past as a*
> *comprehensive heritage or reject it as if it were*
> *mine to reject.*
> *I can identify myself only with modern India.*[28]

But, however, the present-day India, with its unity in diversity gives him all the needful poetic inspirations. Therefore he says:

> *The Indian landscape sears my eyes.*
> *I have become a part of it.*[29]

As William Walsh rightly puts it:

> *Nissim Ezekiel in the Indian scene is a permanent expartriate, but one who has freely elected to stay.*[30]

It is his expatriate objectivity that makes him critical of the Indian scene, with a sense of puckish humour and teasing. He appears to be constantly telling in his poetry, what fools these Indian be? In his poem *The Truth About the Floods,* Ezekiel discusses India as a vast geographical entity, and if there are floods on one part of the country, utter draught is likely to prevail in various other parts. The above poem is a categorical Audenesque satire of an ovccurrence of flood in:

> *Balasore, Mayurbhanj and Cuttack in*
> *North Bihar and Orissa.*[31]

As Nissim Ezekiel puts that it was:

> *A found poem based on a report by V.K. Dixit in* ***The Indian Express****, Bombay 25 September, 1967.*[32]

The expression 'A found poem' is quite intriguing. He puts upon himself the stance of 'a visitor', and it is a job 'to find out the truth'.[33] A flood is always a matter of great natural calamity. Even on the face of such calamity the Indians nurture a highness desire in them to make personal profits out of such disaster. It is a poem that blatantly exposes the Indian tendencies of selfishness greed and aversion. The same selfish joy of fortunate-than-thou attitude is to be found in the relief party that has to do a little bit of social service in the flooded affected area. The very manner of the arrival of relief party speaks for the unfeeling nature of the party. Says Ezekiel:

> *A relief party came at last. Five students*
> *with a transistor,*
> *a tin of biscuits,*
> *a camera.*[34]

In the flood affected area itself hunger and want are making a naked dance. The following lines clarify the unfortunate state of affairs closely following the above lines, we have:

> *The villagers ran to them.*
> *They slapped their bellies and whined:*
> *'I have not eaten for three days.'*
> *'My husband has been washed away.'*
> *'My parents have abandoned me.'*
> *'My son is dying.'*
> *'I cannot find my daughter'.*[35]

The inhuman manner in which the 'relief party' performed itself is to be found in the following lines:

> *'Don't make a noise'.*
> *said the students,*
> *'sit down in a circle.'*
> *The villagers sat down in a circle.*
> *They did not say another word,*
> *The transistor was on,*
> *the biscuits were distributed,*
> *the camera clicked.*
> *Then the students left*
> *humming the tune*
> *of a popular Hindi film song.*[36]

The part played by the government officials themselves is not less inhuman. On reaching the village, the villagers would not tell him anything 'till I told them I wasn't a government official'.[37] The message is obvious. The villagers are not at all convinced about the authentic charitable nature of the government officials. Every official claims that his area was worst hit in the floods. But at the same time, he also gives a very great fake list of the relief work:

Meet any official
he will claim his district,
sub-division or block
is the 'worst-hit',.
and pass on a hand-out
with statistics of relief-work.[38]

When he visited Balasore, at the end all such places, the villagers would not talk to him 'till I told them I wasn't a government official'. The whole scenario is a picture of the cynical performance of fellow humans turning their backs towards the hard hit flood victims. The concluding lines obviously clarify the precautious nature of the government machinery. While they shamelessly expressed that they could not help or could not have done better. The Concluding lines of the poem are as follows:

The district authorities
at Balasore
admitted they had failed,
but they claimed they could not have done
better. Nature, they said,
had conspired against them.
'Write the truth', they said,
'in your report'.
And so I did.[39]

This poem is one more example which envisions the inhuman tendencies of the Indians, particularly in a time of calamity. If the *Night of the Scorpion* reflects at an individual calamity of a particular person, *The Truth about the Floods* tremendously expresses the human mis-behaviour in the context of public calamity.

In fact Ezekiel wants to suggest that Indians had never

developed in themselves a mature machinery zeal to do a little bit of charitable work. Ezekiel's submission that the Indians are still in a primitive stage of helplessness is by and large correct. But, however, he constantly pleads 'for human good humanly got' all through his poems.

Growing Materialism and Corruption of Humanity

In so far as the corrupt morals of humanity are concerned, Nissim Ezekiel does not single out India as such. The growing materialism corrupts the whole world. The same things is expressed by him in his poem*The Double Horror* :

> *I am corrupted by the world, continually*
> *Reduced to something less than human by the crowd,*
> *Newspapers, cinemas, radio features, speeches*
> *Demanding peace by men with grim warlike faces,*
> *Posters selling health and happiness in bottles,*
> *Large returns for small investments, in football pools*
> *Or self-control, six easy lessons for a pound,*
> *Holidays in Rome for writing praise of toothpastes,*
> *The jungle growth of what so obviously intends*
> *To suck life from life, leaving you and me*
> *corrupted.*[40]

It is a matter of common experience that innumerable peripheral even useless items of life are crazily wanted by the people, who think themselves to be civilized. But, Ezekiel looks upon them as to have been 'reduced to something less than human'. 'The newspapers, cinemas, radio features, speeches' are so grim and ironic that they make people confused and corrupted in themselves. But, however, these are so powerful that people ordinarily cannot extricate themselves from these evil propaganda media. Ezekiel further elaborates the corrupting forces of society as 'cheaply enticing features'. He rightly calls well 'the jungle growth of what so obviously intends/to suck life from life'. 'The jungle growth' metaphor intending to 'suck life from life' renders the people obviously incapable of really thinking for themselves. Towards the end of the poem he says that the modern world, with its corrupting forces let loose on the public is the only world in which one is forced to live. Therefore, he concludes the poem as follows:

> *Between the world and me there is a frightful*
> *Equipoise, as infected I corrupt the world.*[41]

The 'frightful equipoise' that he speaks of becomes the angle of objective observations in his poem *In India.* Everyone knows that India is a land of poverty, ignorance and illiteracy. For innumerable centuries it was under the intrigues cornage of the foreign rulers. Demographically speaking the aboriginal Indian culture had always been imbalanced phenomena. As a result of all these atrocities the Indian masses have turned out of to be helpless. They cannot even think of acquiring for themselves a decency and dignity of life. Therefore, the following long list of categories of people are *Suffering the place and time.*[42] The unfortunate helpless people are:

> *. . . the beggars,*
> *Hawkers, pavement sleepers,*
> *Hutment dwellers, slums,*
> *Dead souls of men and gods,*
> *Burnt-out mothers, frightened*

Virgins, wasted child
And tortured animal
All in noisy silence.[43]

The expression 'the noisy silence' is poetically very effective they are silent as they do not have a voice of their own. It is obvious clamour, most needfully made, by these people. Living among them is really a painful experience. But the poetic impulse in him cannot render him insensible to the widespread evils of want and poverty. The poet's own helplessness is stated in the following lines:

Suffering the place and time,
I ride my elephant of thought,
A Cezanne slung around my neck.[44]

It is here that we find the poetic influence of W.H. Auden. In this context, the following words of S.Z.H. Abidi are worth quoting; coming upon the above stanza Abidi says:

> *Ezekiel doesn't glamouries the filth, poverty and squalor that is India. The 'elephant of thought' continues its journey almost unconcerned but not entire unconcerned either, because it is aware of the importance of social conscience that cannot change anything the reference to 'Cezanne' carries within it the echo of the fact of importance.*[45]

Poverty and Helplessness of the Indian Masses

Many of Ezekiel's latter poems such as Poverty Poems' and various others touch upon the unfortunate concerns of Indian life. At the same time, they also reveal his human concerns and sympathy for the Indian masses. Therefore S.Z.H. Abidi adds to the above as follows:

> *His Indianness is a condition of the mind, the product of intellectual and emotional sympathy without a trace of self-consciousness, a kind of identification which may more adequately be termed as spiritual kinship.*[46]

But, however, this 'spiritual kinship' of Nissim Ezekiel becomes localized to the urban India. Therefore, Satya Narian Singh in his *Ramanujan and Ezekiel* says as follows:

> *. . . it is difficult to identify any specific tradition in Ezekiel although some of his poems glimpse forth aspects of urban living in India.*[47]

Ezekiel himself was quite categorical in stating that he prominently belongs to Bombay and its environments, says Ezekiel::

> *I regard myself essentially as an Indian poet writing in English. I have strong sense of belonging, not only to India, but to this city.*[48]

The above vistas of poverty and helplessness are certainly not exclusive for Bombay they are more or less common everywhere in India. In fact, Ezekiel captures the totality of the Indian misfortune. Bombay is a near occasional background. Moreover, his aversion to city is born of the influence of the Western poets like Baudelaire and T.S. Eliot. However, Linda Hess gives the following comprehensive view of his poetry:

> *He (Ezekiel) is a poet of the city,*
> *Bombay; a poet of the body; and an endless*
> *explorer of labyrinths of the mind, the devious*

> *delving and twisting of the ego, and the ceaseless*
> *attempt of man and poet to define himself and*
> *to find through all 'the myth and maze' a way of*
> *honesty and love.*[49]

Ezekiel is positive in stating that a writer invariably needs an identity for himself as he himself says in interview in the *Indian Literary Reveiw*:

> *A writer needs a national or cultural identity,*
> *without that you become a series of imitations,*
> *echoes, responses, but you do not develop,*
> *because there is nothing at the core to develop.*[50]

It is this intention to maintaining him 'a core to deveiop' that Ezekiel ponders deep into the vehement discom-features in the moralities of life as found in Bombay. The Section II of *In India* is a vehement satirical portrait of the divided and conflicting emotional tendencies of the people.

We often hear about unity in diversity as a great virtue of India. It is a land of many religions, many cultures and many speech groups co-existing as one nation. But, however, this kind of co-existing as one nature is a recent historical occurrence in the country. History bears a testimony to the fact that the Indians had been a divided lot in their cultural, and even national contexts in the past. Even in the twentieth century the inner authentic divisions in the minds of the people are a reality. The same reality was brought out by Ezekiel in a very objective and even cynical manner in his poem *In India* as follow:

> *The Roman Catholic Goan boys*
> *The whitewashed Anglo-Indian boys*

The musclebound Islamic boys
Were earnest in their prayers.[51]

It is evident from the above that the Indians are incapable of living as one nation even today. The differences in the minds of the people are marked and clear. Ezekiel's practical anxiety in stating like above is to remind the public that if they are required to live like one nation, they have to do away with the evil differentiating forces of their lives.

Ezekiel's Views About India

Nissim Ezekiel as a poet is not a mere satirist and ironist. He maintains in himself innumerable ideological moorings concerning the future of India. He wants to correct and rectify tendencies of the people in India. Ezekiel's poetry is such corrective force. It brings a salient alteration and conversion in the minds of the readers by way of mirrorizing and magnifying the pitfalls in their personalities and their attitudes. Unless and until we do not make a potential correction in our attitude, we cannot establish the most wanted new nation conceived in equality fraternity and brotherhood. The new representative that we borrowed from the west are not likely to function if we do not alter our traditional attitudes. Only after such an alteration and change we can be able to establish the future India on strong foundation. Ezekiel's poetical animation concerning the future of India are discussed in the next chapter.

REFERENCES

1. P. P. Mehta, 'Nissim Ezekiel', *Contemporary Indo-English Verse, Vol. II (A Collection of Critical Essays on Male Poets)*, ed. A.N. Dwivedi Ed. (Bareilly : Prakash Book Depot, 1984), p. 211.
2. *Ibid.*
3. Nissim Ezekiel, *Latter-Day Psalms* (Delhi: Oxford University Press, 1982), p. 50.
4. Inder Nath Kher, ed., *Journal of South Asian Literature*, Vol. XI, Nos. 3-4 (Spring, Summer 1976), p. 203.
5. Frank Birbal Singh, 'My Being Human' An Interview with Nissim Ezekiel', *Contemporary Indian-English Poetry* Atma Ram ed. (Calcutta: A Writers Workshop Publication, 1989), pp. 180-81.
6. *Ibid.*
7. K. Ayyappa Paniker, 'Beyond Irony: The Third Vision of Nissim Ezekiel', *Indian Literature in English* (Madras: Anu Chithra Publication, 1989), p. 83.
8. William Walsh, 'The Meeting of Language and Literature and the Indian Example', *Writers in East-West Encounter: New, Cultural Bearings*, ed. Guy Amirthanayagam (London: Macmillan, 1982), p. 125.
9. Nissim Ezekiel, *Hymns in Darkness* (Delhi: Oxford University Press, 1976), p. 13.
10. Inder Nath Kher, ed., *Journal of South Asian Literature*, Vol. II, Nos. 3-4 (Spring, Summer 1976), p. 11.
11. *Ibid.*, p. 12.
12. Lakshmi Raghunandan, 'Nissim Ezekiel', *Contemporary Indian Poetry in English* (New Delhi: Reliance Publishing House, 1990), p. 11.
13. Rajeev Taranath and Meena Belliappa, *The Poetry of Nissim Ezekiel* (Calcutta: A Writers Workshop, 1966), p. 14.
14. Nissim Ezekiel, *Latter-Day Psalms* (Delhi: Oxford University Press, 1982), p. 49.
15. *Ibid.*
16. *Ibid.*
17. *Ibid.*, p. 50.

18. *Ibid.*
19. Rajeev Taranath and Meena Belliappa, *The Poetry of Nissim Ezekiel* (Calcutta: A Writers Workshop, 1966), p. 14.
20. M. K. Naik, 'The Tale is in the Sting: An Analysis of Ezekiel's "Night of the Scorpion", *Dimensions of Indian English Literature* (New Delhi: Sterling Publishers Pvt. Ltd., 1984), p. 35.
21. Christopher Wiseman, 'The Development of Technique in the Poetry of Nissim Ezekiel', *Contemporary Indian English Verse: An Evaluation*, ed. Chirantan Kulshrestha (New Delhi : Arnold Heinemann, 1980), p. 145.
22. Nissim Ezekiel, *Hymns in Darkness* (Delhi: Oxford University Press, 1976), p. 11.
23. *Ibid.*
24. *Ibid.*
25. *Ibid.*, p. 13.
26. *Ibid.*
27. Inder Nath Kher, ed., *Journal of South Asian Literature*, Vol. XI, Nos. 3-4 (Spring, Summer 1976), p. 147.
28. Nissim Ezekiel, 'Naipaul's India and Mine', *New Writing in India*, ed. Adil Jusswala (Harmondsworth, 1974), pp. 88-89.
29. Nissim Ezekiel, *Hymns in Darkness* (Delhi: Oxford University Press, 1976), p. 13.
30. William Walsh, 'The Indian Sensibility in English', *Awakened Conscience: Studies in Commonwealth Literature*, ed. C.D. Narasimhaish Ed. (New Delhi: Sterling Publishers, 1978), pp. 68-69.
31. Nissim Ezekiel, *Hymns in Darkness* (Delhi: Oxford University Press, 1976), p. 19.
32. *Ibid.*
33. *Ibid.*
34. *Ibid.*, p. 20.
35. *Ibid.*
36. *Ibid.*
37. *Ibid.*, p. 21.
38. *Ibid.*, p. 19.
39. *Ibid.*, p. 21.

40. Inder Nath Kher, ed., *Journal of South Asian Literature,* Vol. XI, Nos. 3-4 (Spring. Summer 1976), p. 14.
41. *Ibid.*
42. Nissim Ezekiel, *Latter-Day Psalms* (Delhi: Oxford University Press, 1982). p. 52.
43. *Ibid.,* p. 50.
44. *Ibid.*
45. S.Z.H. Abidi, *Studies in Indo-Anglian Poetry* (Bareilly: Prakash Book Depot, 1979), p. 229.
46. *Ibid.,* p. 287.
47. Satyanarain Singh, 'Ramanujan and Ezekiel', *Contemporary Indian English Verse: An Evaluation,* ed. Chirantan Kulshrestha (New Delhi: Arnold Heinemann, 1980), p. 165.
48. S.Z.H. Abidi, *Studies in Indo-Anglian Poetry* (Bareilly: Prakash Book Depot, 1979), p. 291.
49. Linda Hess, 'Post Independence Indian Poetry in English', *Quest,* No. 49 (Spring, 1966), p. 30.
50. 'Interview with Nissim Ezekiel', *Indian Literary Review,* Vol. I, No. X (February, 1979).
51. Nissim Ezekiel, *Latter-Day Psalms* (Delhi: Oxford University Press, 1982), p. 50.

6

Towards a Real Brave New World

Nissim Ezekiel's main idea of writing poetry appears to be the establishment of a brave new world. In this world of Ezekiel personal authenticities should reign supreme and not the traditions and conventions. Ezekiel constantly celebrates in his poetry what Henry James called 'the "vulgarity" entranced in the heart of modern civilization'.[1] This he does with a stern purpose of rectifying the otherwise bizarre and inhuman sensibilities of the individuals. The individual human sensibilities, according to Ezekiel went astray and irrational because of the excessive craving for materialistic comforts and luxuries.

Impressionistic Poetic Technique

Precisely speaking Ezekiel exposes the silly manner in which the individual senses and sensibilities are going absolutely uncorrelated and uncoordinated with his authentic sense of being. The interesting point that Ezekiel stresses in this connection is in his pecksniffian manner of turning against himself, by way of making himself the poetical target of his satire and criticism. The ironic manner in which he equivalizes the Poet, the Lover and the Birdwatcher has already been discussed at length in the second chapter. Using the modern techniques of impressionistic poetic technology he describes himself as to how the world's appearances and illusions as a sensual phenomena turns him into an enthusiastic devotee of the petty human passions of Libido in his parnographic *Nude Poems*. More then in the *Nude Poems* there are a few examples in the *Poster Prayers*. The skeptical and ironic manner of his prayers become explicit in the following poems:

Do not choose me, O Lord.
to carry out thy purposes.
I'm quite worthy, of course,
but I have my own purposes.
You have plenty of volunteers
to choose from, Lord,
Why pick on me, the selfish one?
O well, if you insist,
I'll do your will.
Please try to make it coincide with mine.[2]

The line 'You have plenty of volunteers/to choose from, Lord', is a mock presentation of his ironic devotional sentiment. Ezekiel is of the view that all serious manners of religious prayers and devotions are absolutely hypocritical and man shows his hypocritical piety rather than his earnest seriousness in pretending to be making prayers. It is interesting to note here that Ezekiel is under scoring the sublime devotional sentiments of John Milton, the Puritan, when he said in his *On His Blindness* as follows:

'Doth God exact day-labour, light denied?'
I fondly ask. But Patience, to prevent
That murmur, soon replies, 'God doth not need'
Either man's work or his own gifts. Who best
Bear his mild yoke, they serve him best. His state
is kingly: thousands at his bidding speed And
post o'er land and ocean without rest.[3]

The lofty sentiments of John Milton are countered by Ezekiel in a humorous manner. The last line 'Please try to make it coincide with mine' reflects at his skeptical manners of half seriously and mockingly bargaining with God. Ezekiel, some how, progressively turned ironic in his devotions towards God and traditions. It is not right to say, along with V.A. Shahane that in his later poems, Ezekiel's poetry:

> *. . . may be described as religious, moral and philosophical and which, incidentally, also indicates the most recent phase of his creative writings.*[4]

Shahane arrives at a lopsided ciritical conclusion finally when he says as follows:

> *Ezekiel's poetry projects his beliefs meaningfully in relations to the posture of the believer and his practices.*[5]

Rightly speaking Ezekiel never adopted for himself, 'the posture of the believer' leave aside 'his (believers) practices'. Shahane intelligently concludes his essay that Ezekiel:

> *. . . poetry explores this existential realm of his beliefs.*[6]

While Ezekiel's existential dilemmas are true, it is not possible to believe that he adopts for himself 'the posture of the believer and his practices', looking to the mass of his skeptical, critical, and oppositional poetry, it is absolutely wrong to arrive at a conclusion that Ezekiel achieved for himself a religious conversion towards the later phases of his poetical life.

Ezekiel is a humorist and his humour becomes abundantly laugh-worthy, when he turns against himself and adopts for himself the mock-believer's postures. Ezekiel right from the beginning suspected all faiths and beliefs. He expects his readers to be conscious of their inner authentic worth of being In the world. It is for the purpose of establishing a courage to be in the world that he propagates the existential manner of living ones own life. His poetry is a guiding force towards that end.

Humour and Irony in the Very Indian Poems in Indian English

Ezekiel's satire on the Indian life and its polity takes a very humorous turn in his *Very Indian Poems in Indian English.* Referring to the self-proclaimed sense of belonging to India by Ezekiel, K. Raghavendra Rao in his article 'The Alienation Games: The Poetry of Nissim Ezekiel' argues in a different way. Says K.R. Rao as follows:

> *The alienation that arises from Ezekiel's communal identity is only one of the alienation games life has forced him to play. As we say, the poet attempts to overcome this alienation by a fatalistic and contemptuous acceptance of the overwhelmingly Hindu environment.*[7]

It is a certain fact that Ezekiel all through his life maintains a certain emotional affinity and identity with India. His realistic and ironic view of India and certain section of its people, particularly in urban scenario, should not be considered as 'alienation that arises from Ezekiel's communal identity'.

Moreover, to charge him with a fatalistic and contemptuous acceptance of the 'over whelming Hindu environment' amounts to play foul with logic and argumentation. Ezekiel's realism and ironic attitude of looking at things does not spare even the Jews. Ezekiel's poem 'Jewish Wedding in Bombay' is a very humorous poem; and it can be concluded as a shrewd poetic observation of the comedy of poetic realism of marriage. K. Raghavendra Rao was properly answered by S.Z.H. Abidi closely commenting after the above extract, says as follows:

> *The fact is that there is no question of alienation for Ezekiel despite his foreign origin. This is a distinguishing feature of his poetry as a whole, the originating impulse behind which is one of affirmation of the Indian milieu with all its paradoxes.*[8]

Moreover, Ezekiel has always maintained a typical gravity of an objective observer and 'the Indian milieu with all paradoxes' becomes a certain theme of his poetry. It is these paradoxes that recieve an acid touch of realism and irony in his hands. But, however, they do not condescend to bitterness and paining satire. The basic paradoxical nature of Indian milieu concerns with its orthodox mentality, coupled with poverty and helplessness. While it is a fact that in these poems he gets preoccupied with the common place and the seemingly insignificant.[9] Further A. Rahman confirms his ideas when he says:

> *It appears that he is more concerned with the sub-human conditions and in such poems, his attitude is basically sympathetic but he turns a bitter critic of our hypocritical and insincere ways at the same time.*[10]

The Very Indian Poems in Indian English constitute an interesting ironic portraits of average lifestyle in India. The manner in which the so-called Indian English, as against the standard English, is handled in these poems is quite funny if not humorous. India is a land of many language. Every language has its own syntactical and phonetics peculiarities. When it comes to the question of gaining perfection in a foreign language, the non-conspicuous syntactical and phonetic features of the mother tongue, invariably enter into the vocable modalities of the said foreign language. English is learnt in India as a second language. To some extent there is a sort of uniformity in the whole of India when it comes to the question of writing it. But in its spoken state the English gets particularly crumpled with the non-conspicuous phonetic features of the various first language or the mother tongues. As a result the English spoken in different parts and different speech island of India communicates differently; and the differences are invariably felt in hearing English spoken. The English people not only introduced the academic institutions, but also rendered it a communicative language of the elite in the public. So to speak English rightly or wrongry turned out to be an 'effected fashion', particularly in middle and upper middle classes.

Peculiarities of Indian Spoken English

In his essay 'Naipaul's India and Mine', referring to the irritating attitude of V.S. Naipaul towards India, Ezekiel points out three important irritants. They are:

> *. . . his reckless generalization, his grotesque exaggeration, his nagging, irritable manner.*[11]

What Ezekiel expects of Naipaul is a little bit of sympathy towards the Indian people:

> *. . . education and cultural limitations their sense of dignity and worth, their humanity, in short.*[12]

But, at the same time, while he does not disagree with Naipaul about the unfortunate state of affairs in the Indian culture, Ezekiel's disagreement is particularly Naipaul's :

> *. . . mode of argument, his falsifying examples.*[13]

The following words of Ezekiel are required to be taken quite seriously:

> *Let me pause to explain again that I see India in most ways as Naipaul see her. All that he says against the grossness and squalor of Indian life, the routine ritualism, the lip-service to high ideals, the petrified and distorted sense of cleanliness, and thousand other things, all this is true.*[14]

In his *Very Indian Poems in Indian English* Ezekiel himself submits all the above negative characteristic features of the Indian people. He makes selective example of typically self-confounded characteristic features and mannerisms of certain people. It is worth noting here that Ezekiel does not make a generalized statement of all Indians, a typical cynical mistake committed by V.S. Naipaul. The truth is some of the Indians, because of their educational and cultural limitations, behave themselves quite unbecomingly, particularly in their physical and verbal gestures in conversing with others. Ezekiel considers these unfortunate types just out of fun, and not out of any malice or venum.

The most important poem that can be taken as an example is 'The Patriot' taken from *Very Indian Poems in Indian English*. Ezekiel gives here an average picture of an Indian, who is a self-styled intellectual. The mere verbal manner of his rambling from the world problems to the national problem through his own personal problems, is quite humorous caricature. He initiates 'The Patriot' as follows:

I am standing for peace and non-violence.
Why world is fighting fighting
Why all people of world
Are not following Mahatma Gandhi,
I am simply not understanding.
Ancient Indian Wisdom is 100% correct.
I should say even 200 % correct.
But Modern generation is neglecting –
Too much going for fashion and foreign things.[15]

The whole poem is a humorous dramatic monologue, which turns against the speaker himself, and exposes the shallowness of his concerns. In spite of the fact that he is a very common man who is incapable of either changing or rectifying the ways of the world, takes the honorific manner of verbally touching at the problems of 'peace and non-violence'. The world 'not following Mahatma Gandhi' and the 'ancient Indian wisdom' is 100 per sent correct, etc. He speaks as though he is plentifully troubled when the 'modern generation is neglecting' the 'ancient Indian Wisdom' and 'too much giving for fashion and foreign things'.

The most important thing here concerns with the incongruous manner in which he speaks English and the affected tyranny of syntax, the curt and cut and dry inauthentic manner in which the protagonist speaks is reminiscent of Zwinglism, after that notorious character Zwingle in *The Pickwick Papers of Charles Dickens.* While Zwingle speaks in gross colloquial dialectic baroque phrases. without bothering for syntax or connectives, the protagonist of Ezekiel here goes to the extent of colloquial sing the English idioms into the Indian language modals.

At the same time, he potentially hints at how he reads *The Times of India* everyday in order to improve his English language, closely justopposing his concern at:

How one goonda fellow
Throw stone at Indirabehn.[16]

The disconnect manner of his speech reaches the humorous heights when he repeats Marks Anthony's initial words of his famous speech in *Julius Caesar of Shakespeare*:

Friends, Romans, Countrymen, I am saying
(to myself)
Lend me the ears.
Everything is coming –
Regeneration, Remuneration, Contraception.[17]

Towards the end of the section he assures the people with the following statement:

> *Be patiently, brothers and sisters.*[18]

The whole portrait becomes vibrant in being callous when he talks of 'prospects of world peace', with:

> *Pakistan behaving like this,*
> *China behaving like that, ...*[19]

Then he dotes upon the brotherhood of humanity; 'all men are brothers, no?'[20] The manner in which the question tag gets appended shows his lack of real perception of the spoken English. So finally he concludes that:

> *Gujaraties, Maharashtrians, Hindiwallahs*
> *All Brothers –* [21]

In this funny manner he comes to conclude his vibrant madness. He assures that inspite of our funny habits,

> *Still, you tolerate me,*
> *I tolerate you.*[22]

This kind of verbal pollution is not uncommon in the linguistic encounters in India. The half-educated muddle heads thinks it a great privilege in speaking English in their own way, without any rule or rim. They brave to do so because of the fact, that some how, all are veritably bad in English. The multi-lingual cultural confluence of India gives them a false notion that the descriptive English has to be spoken, or is spoken, in that verigated and reckless manner only. All this emerges because of the false notion that speaking English is in itself a matter of status in India. It was rulers language up to 1947 which unfortunately turned into an official language after Independence. What Ezekiel wants to suggest is that Indians have a typical characteristic trait of verbally imposing themselves in all situations, even when their very presence is a mere non-entity? It has yet to be statistically verified as to how many half educated Indians entering into a frail and useless chatter because of their inferiority complex provoking them to be superior in the social and cultural encounters. This inferiority complex itself stems from their own self-supposed notions of their own mother tongue being inferior to English. The Puckish manner in which Ezekiel elicits his reflection of 'What fools these Indians are, they kill English while they speak it'. An average Indian is of immense nuisance value because of his self-supposed mastery of English language.

The other important poem in this context is *The Professor*. The poem presents the dramatic situation of a super-annuated professor coming into a chance encounter with one of his old student. The poem is a verbal conversational declamation starting with the interrogative and intimidative doubts, with the following expression:

Remember me? I am Professor Sheth.[23]

Despite the fact that the Very Indian Poems in Indian English are written with an exclusive casual purpose of creating a light-hearted humour, they are containing in them certain typical oddities of human behaviour exclusively pursuable in the dispositions of the people in the subcontinent. Average Indians have a typical weakness of aiming at figuring high in the estimations of others. This may be partly due to their original feudal background, in which they imaginatively self-styled themselves as lords and ladies and partly because of their in-bred, again self-supposed, inferiority complex.

The very title *The Professor* suggestively indicates the complacent manner in which the protagonist presents himself as a high profiled personage. He is a retired professor; and on encountering one of his old student he becomes vibrant in his chatter, in the context of which he graphically makes a revelation of his life achievements in a very proud manner. But, quite ironically the entire text of his revelation becomes a boring rambling and that too quite unoccasional. It is just possible that this retired professor, who taught geography once, is typically a super-annuated chatter-box. Whether it is occasional or otherwise he always seems to have certain important things of his life to tell others. This is a mere egotistical sublime in its bathetic dimensions. He says about his retirement in spite of his good health, about his children, two of whom are settled as:

> *One is Sales Manager,*
> *One is Bank Manager,*
> *Both have cars.*
> *Other also doing well, though not so well.*[24]

The professor designates the third one as a 'Black sheep' for doing 'not so well as his other children'. His two daughters were married to 'very nice boys'; he was quite proud in stating that he had eleven grand children in spite of the fact 'these are the days of family planning'; and he compliments this old student for having just three children.

Then he immediately stretched himself philosophically that,

> *We have to change with times.*
> *Whole world is changing. In India also*
> *We are keeping up.*[25]

Then he talks of 'Old values are going, new values are coming'.[26] Again he reverts back to 'old age'. In spite of the fact his 'health was O.K. usual aches and pains', he does not have any serious health hazards like:

> *No diabetes, no blood pressure, no heart attack.*
> *This is because of sound habits in youth.*[27]

The concluding portion of the poem extends an invitation to the student stating that:

> *I am living just on opposite house's backside.*[28]

The whole chatter smacks of irrelevance, condescending to nonsense in the mind of his old student. He keeps silent all through, for fear of being forced to many more lectures of his professor, if encountered with a verbal response. The professor asks him to visit his 'humble residence also' if the students was 'coming again this side by chance'. In spite of the fact that his residence was just on the back of the opposing house, the manner in which he invites the student any other time if he was 'coming again this side by chance', is quite unmannerly on his part. He could as well have asked him to peep into his house at the moment also. But, in a typical Indian manner he does not want to entertain guests in his home, even though he prefers to bore them on the road side with his typical irrelevant manner of speaking English. The expressions like 'In India also we are keeping up', 'Our progress is progressing', 'Old values are going' new values are coming', 'this year I am sixtynine and hope to score century', 'You are so thin, like a stick', 'Coming again this side, living opposite just back side' are typical Indianism literally rendered into terse English of the bookish sort. It is absolutely the manner of his speech that irritates. This is more or less, 'the case of all Indians who learn English as a second language, without ever being introduced to the native English speech Islands. Ezekiel makes a laughable joke of the manner in which English is spoken by the Indians.

The 'Irani Restaurant Instructions' is another typical Indian English poem. The poem is supposed to be a display chart on the wall about what the customer should not do in the restaurant. It is just possible that people come to the restaurant to write letters, to make their hair brushed, and make mischiefs of all sorts. The instructions strictly forbid them:

> *Do not write letter*
> *without order refreshment.*[29]

Slipping the article where it is necessary is a usual mistake instead of 'a letter' simply 'letter' is used. To be right it should have been 'a letter' or 'letters' again in the imperative mood it should always be spoken 'don't' and not literal 'do not'; and then in the next lines it should have been 'ordering refreshment' the noun order is used as a verbal. The next instruction is in reference to the odd habits of Indians who go to comb their hair in all public places, thinking of presenting themselves trim and beautiful. Therefore, the instruction is:

Do not comb
Hair is spoiling floor.[30]

The other casual visitors to the restaurant are the mischief mongers. It is stated 'don't make mischief in cabin'. The expression 'making mischiefs' is probably an Indian expression of forbidding them from making love in the cabins. It is stated the waiter 'Our waiter is reporting'. With such forbidding notes on the wall. The concluding part of the poem is quite humorous. They are asked to report the matter 'if not satisfied tell us'. The statements goes, like this 'if not satisfied tell us, otherwise tell others'. This is quite humorous termination of the poem.

The very Indian poems of Ezekiel are casual humorous exercises. With such poetic exercises Ezekiel voices forth both the serious side of life, as well as the uncultured dimensions of it, without any reservation or inhibition. As a matter of fact, Ezekiel is absolutely frustrated with the ignorance, illiteracy, and culturelessness of the Indian masses. Both the urban and sub-urban areas are equally bad in this respect. He exposes the urban with a lashing satire and expresses the sub-urban with a sense of pity and sympathy for the helplessness and ignorance of the people.

Ezekiel always aimed at high values in life in the post-Independence context. India is struggling to remain unified and signified as a nation, but the behaviour and norms of the people are typically unconcerned.

It is this unconcern on the part of the people of India that makes Ezekiel sick at his heart. He maintains in himself a sincere vision of life which must go to make a nation as a cultured and civilized unit.

REFERENCES

1. Nina Baym, *The Norton Anthology of American Literature* (New York: W. W. Norton & Compnay, 1980), p. 1384.
2. Inder Nath Kher, ed., *Journal* of *South Asian Literature,* Vol. XI, Nos. 3-4 (Spring, Summer 1976), p. 134.
3. Monroe C. Beardsley, *Theme and Form: An Introduction to Literature* (New Jersey' Prentice Hall, 1973), p. 638.
4. Inder Nath Kher, ed., *Journal* of *South Asian Literature,* Vol. XI, Nos. 3-4 (Spring, Summer 1976), p. 253.
5. *Ibid.,* p. 261.
6. *Ibid.*
7. K. Raghavendra Rao, 'The Alienation Games: The Poetry of Nissim Ezekiel', *Prespectives on Indian Poetry in English,* ed. M.K. Naik, (New Delhi: Abhinav Publication 1984), p. 102.
8. S.Z.H. Abidi, *Studies in Indo-Anglian Poetry* (Bareilly : Prakash Book Dept, 1987), p. 291.
9. *Ibid.* p. 82.
10. Inder Nath Kher, ed., *Journal* of *South Asian Literature,* Vol. XI, Nos. 3-4 (Spring, Summer 1976), p. 196.
11. *Ibid.*
12. *Ibid.,* p. 201.
13. *Ibid.*
14. Nissim Ezekiel, *Latter-Day Psalms* (Delhi: Oxford University Press, 1982), p. 22.
15. *The Patriot,* p. 22.
16. *Ibid.*
17. *Ibid.*
18. Ibid.
19. Nissim Ezekiel, *Latter-Day Psalms* (Delhi: Oxford University Press, 1982), p. 23.
20. *The Patriot,* p. 23.
21. *Ibid.*
22. *Ibid.*
23. *The Professor,* p. 23.

24. *Ibid.*
25. *Ibid.*, p. 24.
26. *Ibid.*
27. *Ibid.*
28. *Ibid.*
29. *Irani Restaurant Instructions*, p. 24.
30. *Ibid.*

7
Conclusion

Nissim Ezekiel is a harsh and bitter critic of the practical applicational aspects of the institutional norms and traditions. So to say he is not against the age old institutions and their prerogatives. When, in the applicational directions the very fundamental purpose of the institutions and traditions gets defeated or even sabotaged he becomes inconsolable upset, and the resultant poetry of Ezekiel turns out to be a broad critcism of life. For this purpose he does not assume upon himself the stance of a rebel. He is intriguingly intellectual and strategically expressive of his bitter feelings. Therefore, his harshness and bitterness takes the form of a persuasive critic, wherein both the harshness and bitterness get sugarcoated in the stylistic properties of his poetry. His *Unfinished Man* is very often looked upon as a formula of romantic nostalgia, elegiacally suggesting the prospects possibility of evolution into a finished man.

The Need of a New World

Nissim Ezekiel starts his exodus into poetry with a profound notion as follows:

The sky
Is smaller than this open eye.[1]

The above line form the concluding submission of his poem *Subject of Change.* It is in this poem that he 'foresaw/ The fury of my inner law'.[2] He at length, talks about the fury of inner law consoling him, otherwise, probably inconsolable as :

Not a stone in the edifice,
Well-loved, is likely to suffice.[3]

Therefore,

Everything calls for a new place
....
The evening walk proved not to be
Along the shore of memory.[4]

The shore of poetry along with the walks is new, and calls for 'a different rage behind my face'.[5] The 'evening walk' metaphor which he uses for his journey into the poetic world is not a mere stuff of imagination. There is clear indication that the human past, however great might it have been, does not suffice his different poetic 'rage'. The different 'rage' that he speaks in tune with the changing modalities of poetic approaches all over the world in our time. In the 'evening walk' metaphor as well as the in-felt 'different rage' passion may appear to be age old romantic orgy. While it is certainly true that he was strongly influenced by the British Romantics Ezekiel's poetic idiom is often akin with that of the moderns more particularly Lord Byron and the Byronic heroics. The fundamental spirit of his poetry is to be found in the fact that it is a medium of his personal experience. This essentially proves that he moving closer to the modern symbolists and imagists, like Baudelaire, T.S. Eliot and Ezra Pound. To that extent he makes a modest claim that he is the innovator of this new poetry in India, when he talks of 'the fury of my inner law'. He shares the modernists' rebellion.

The new poetry of Ezekiel is a ruthless criticism of society and life as he found it for himself. Ezekiel's social and cultural concerns are obvious. But more obvious are his personal convictions concerning the objective world of his experience. This objective world of experience is both traditional and modern. It is traditional to the extent that it smacks the age-old backwardness of the social institutions like family, nation, society and the like. It is modern in the sense that it at length depends upon the inter-personal relation between man and woman in a frank atmosphere of freedom and choice, even when it comes to smashing the old world in order to establish the new one. Precisely speaking Ezekiel looks upon the glorious human traditions from the point of view of a modernist, and looks upon the content of modernism itself from what it constitutes as permanent in the fundamental human institutions. This permanence is to be found in humanism which is both old and new. The contingent essence of his poetry is like a criticism of life, both old and new.

Ezekiel is essentially a critic of culture. At the same time, he endorses for himself the great purpose of a poet as a creator of certain new values of life for himself. Critics at length have been talking about his craft of poetry. In so far as poet craft is concerned he never makes a pretence of originality. He gracefully admitted:

> *. . . that Pound, Eliot, Yeats, Rilke, Macneice, Spender, Auden and Modern Americans, poetry in general have been the major influences on him.*[6]

The poetic techniques of all the above poets are faithfully implemented by Ezekiel. But, however, it is not right to conclude that often it is a profound analogy rather than a slavish imitation. As a critic of cultures, human values, and the social institutions, it is not the craft of his poetry that matters much. In fact, he assumes for himself a rare vigour and force, coupled with a little bit of irony and humour, in order to bring home his poetic purpose. The originality of Ezekiel remains with his poetic force which is colloquial and conversational. His critical posture are again borrowed from the modern Western philosophers like Martin, and Heideger and the phenomenological critics. Ezekiel always aspires for a balance between human sense and sensibility, as against the presumptuous philosophical and mystical pursuits of the traditionalists. Life's clarity' of purpose is in living with a sort of conscious awareness of being-in-the-world. It does not mean to imply that he is a violent revolutionary. He is just a persuasive pragmatist. At the best he is a balanced personality. Therefore, he asserts that:

> *I am at clarity above all, claim never to have return on obsure form. I like to make controlled, meaningful statement avoiding extremes of thought and expression.*[7]

The clarity which he speaks about concerns with the clarity of human existence. In order to drive his point home he may often ironically turns against himself, and proposes a sort of picture which turns out to be a caricature. But the caricaturist stand is not always backed up. In his poem *Poet, Lover, Birdwatcher* he aims at striking at exploring 'the heart's dark floor'. This poem had highly been acclaimed 'as the greatest landmark of Ezekiel's poetry'. In a way the poem aims at striking at the glorious assertion that the poems are found and they are not made. This is certainly a romantic credo. But Ezekiel attributes a realistic turn when he tries to find the similarity in life purposes of a *Poet, Lover and Birdwatcher*. The inclusion of Birdwatcher here is quite interesting. Shakespeare long ago asserted that poet, lover and the lunatic 'are of imagination all compact'.[8] Ezekiel substitutes 'the lunatic' with the 'Birdwatcher'. It is at once humorous and ludicrous as a parallel. While Shakespeare himself aimed at a little bit of humour when he said so, Ezekiel might not be repeating the same sentiments. How does a Birdwatcher claim simultaneity along with 'a poet and a lover' as had been claimed by Bijay Kumar Das? If the 'Birdwatcher' is a mere ornithologist the simultaneity falls flat. We have the synonym for 'birdwatcher' in the 'Birdcatcher'. In the oriental context a 'birdcatcher' is always considered to be a cruel creature. But, however, he has an instinctive purpose of catching the bird and satisfying his hunger. A poet's need for a poem is probably such an instinctive desire. The craft worth of a birdcatcher and the craft worth of lover and poet find simultaneously in their desires of hunger. While:

> *. . . the women slowly turn around,*
> *Not only flesh and bone but myths of light*
> *With darkness at the core.*[9]

For a lover as well as for a poet the poem too had both the sublime and heightening meaning. Ezekiel wants to strike at the point that the sublime itself turns bathetic in life after the sublime movement, i.e. after the purpose is fulfilled. So coming to the 'Birdwatcher' instance the bird which usually soars high in the sky ultimately turns out to be a mere one time meal after the entire purpose of catching is over. Here is the significant metaphoric point that Ezekiel instates that:

> *and sense is found*
> *By poets lost in crooked, restless flight.*[10]

is expressive of his sense of waste in pursuing a poem. It was Wallace Stevens who said that 'a poem comes to words, just as a tree comes to twings'.[11] At the end of the poem Ezekiel adds a formal traditional cliches of the Hindi devotional poets. Says Ezekiel 'the deaf can hear, the blind recover sight'.[12] This appendix his ironic dimensions. It may all be true about the deaf and the blind. But what about the normal in stating that the myths of life are the precious finding of a lover, so much so the 'birdwatcher' and a 'poet' also after pursuing 'crooked restless flights' arrives at the same kind of frustration. The very first three lines are indicative of Ezekiel's irony. Ezekiel wants to suggests that the best poet waits for words. What are these words and we have that linguistic proposition that all words are metaphors. If so they too are myths. However, the words as well as myths of life are to be caught instantly and instinctively. In fact, he pleads for slow and precautious movements in all walks of life. Those who hurry up and work with haste may create clowns out of themselves. The best poet always wait just like a lover and a birdwatcher. But his waiting is not at all a guarantee that the best poem comes out of this waiting. Ezekiel appears to be convincing himself to the idea the world's best poem has not yet been written. Such is the ironic purpose of Ezekiel; and he pursues his poet-craft with this ironic slant, coupled with tongue in the cheek humour. To be a poet in the modern times, with so much of man-made destruction around, is not at all a happy vocation on the other hand, it is a painful task. This is what T.S. Eliot voiced forth in the concluding lines of *The Wasteland*:

> *Datta*   *Dayadhvam*   *Damyata*
> *Shantih*   *shantih*   *shantih.*[13]

Ezekiel's poem *Poet, Lover and Birdwatcher* to the extent that it is mock heroic and ironic, reflects at the painful manner of taking up poetry as a vocation.

The Purpose of Ezekiel's Writing

In the essay 'Nissim Ezekiel–Pilgrimage and Myth', Michael Garman introduces a unique point of importance concerning Ezekiel as a poet:

> *He is a poet of whom it is not trivial to say that his poetry and his life are inextricable, and whose purpose in writing is to make a harmony (life, poetry) out of a purely biological fact (existence).*[14]

Life in its higher sense, that is poetry and life in practical sense, is purely a biological factor of existence, of seeing antitheticals. As a matter of fact all poetry, in the sense of personally experiencing life in its minute particulars, is always a matter of personal crisis. Life has to be lived that is to be existed in the minute particulars, of personal experiences. It is also to be comprehended and confirmed into an abstraction, the very act of which ultimately becomes poetical in the higher sense. Recognizing the mutual forces of attraction between life and poetry is in itself an act of appreciatory criticism, in experience.

In the practical life of everybody for a self-endorsed introspection there is always that abstraction called life which binds the everyday experiences to the being. And this type of harmonizing extraction into a poem invariably proposes a critical act of looking life itself as a concerned agent. Such concerned agent is Nissim Ezekiel and for him the harmonized continuation of life is always rediscovered in a line or a phrase; an idea or an image. He conforms the fact that these lines are phrases and ideas or images are copious reminders of the continuity of life. Therefore, this continuity of life is all important. In his preface to the second volume of *Sixty Poems* he states as follows:

> *I must confess that my main reason for publishing these sixty poems is that I have not the courage to destroy them. There is in each a line or phrase, an idea or image which helps me to maintain some sort of continuity in my life. If I could transcend the personal importance of these poems I would not publish them. I am interested in writing poetry not in making a personal verse record.*[15]

If we take a critical examination of his concept of 'continuity of life' these images that contain a rare sense and feeling of living the personal movements of existence with a heightened sense of satisfaction and fulfilment. The ultimate source of this satisfaction and fulfilment is life itself in its innumerable and inexhaustable particulars. For Ezekiel these particulars are all significant and they are more important than a mere composed poem itself. This is so because of the simple fact that the real enhalncing forces of life as a property worth living is to be found in the elusive felt experiences and illusory properties of living movements of life. Since these living movements are practically inexhaustible poetry itself, which is made up of these life particulars is elusive. Therefore, says Ezekiel:

But poetry is elusive; to write a
poem is comparatively easy.[16]

The obvious simplistic manner in which he says writing poetry 'is comparatively easy', is in itself a suggestion that the exact living of life in its heightened sense of enjoying the particulars of life is more difficult than writing about them. It is in everybody's experience that life even in its crude particulars offers none the chance of heightenings and sublimations. If so there is more poetry in the life lived than in the poetic forms composed. However, these poetic forms are important in the sense that they bring back the felt particulars of life to the memory; and thus they go to establish what Ezekiel calls the 'continuity of life'. The same point he declares in his poem *Poetry* in his volume *A Time to Change:*

A poem is an episode, completed
In an hour or two, but poetry
Is something more. It is the why
The how, the what, the flow

From which a poem comes,
In which the savage and the singular,
The gentle, familiar.
Are all dissolved, the residue
Is what you read, as a poem, the rest
Flows and is poetry.[17]

'The rest flows' is in itself a confirmation of the fact that there is a rare continuity in life; and it is worth living for that continuity. A poem is a mere artifice which helps to establish 'the continuity of life'.

Poetic Process: Continuity of Life

Life is a rare blend of emotions, feelings and imagination which are circumstantially important in being the reminders of the continuation of life. These feeling emotions and imagination are natural product of existence. To that extent they are common place and ordinary. But when they become the forces of poetic reaction they assume for themselves a rare strength and heightening of what Ezekiel calls the 'rest flows'. This rest that flows is what he calls pure poetry; and in being so it helps to establish the continuity of life. Therefore, poetry is all important. What Ezekiel calls poetry is not limited to the poems on hand. Each and every poem of Ezekiel contains in itself a significant gesture towards what he calls the poetic process of continuity. In adopting this poetic process of continuity for himself, he profoundly improvizes such quickening forces of operation through certain phrases, images, symbols and all such process of continuity of life in the observation of life particulars around.

William Empson in his 'Seven Types of Ambiguities' makes a copious mention of what originates a poetic process. Says Empson:

> *Unexplained beauty arouses an irritation in me.*[18]

What constitutes 'beauty' or otherwise is always a matter of personal judgement depending upon the concerned situation. The thing itself, with all its potential for reaction in the observer, is a matter of initiation for the observer until and unless a sort of self-confounded answer for the mystery gets conceived. The things in the universe are not only mysterious but also inexhaustible. However, the most feasible analogy of interpretation arrived at by the poet on the instance is only a momentary timely answer for the things mystery. The thing itself is likely to remain mysterious as an object of wonder. It remains permanently ingrained and for all times elluding the grasp of a poet. In the mean time what a poet makes out of his raport with the things in themselves, when conformed into analogies, images, symbols and phrases it is a poem; and according to Ezekiel it is 'easier to write a poem'.[19] However, the task of writing a poem becomes easier when the right symbols, images and phrases occur to the poet. Michael Garman rightly puts as:

> *The making of poetry out of existence is the highest synthesis possible, and what Ezekiel declares himself to be aiming at.*[20]

Expressionistic Technique

In his poem *On the Bellasis Road* Ezekiel at length substantiates his point as to how an object of wonder throws him into a fit of passion of creativity. Says Ezekiel:

I see her first
as colour only,
poised against the faded
red of a post-box:
purple sari, yellow blouse,
green bangles, orange
flowers in her hair.
A moment later
I sense her as woman
bare as her feet
beneath the shimmer.[21]

The word 'Bellasis' in the title is quite intriguing. 'Bella' in the sense of 'a beautiful woman' suggests at the road, where such a woman is there on the road. At the outset, he saw her from a distance; and in spite of her exotic dress, ornaments and decorations she appeared to him as 'colour' only. The faded nature of the 'post-box' explains the confusion. The muf of the post-box got mixed up or shadowed by the exotic decoration in which the 'Bella' adumbrates herself. When she is poised against the faded red of a post-box, that in itself rouses a curiosity. The people usually post their letters in the post-box and go away. But this 'Bella' had 'poised' herself against the post-box, which is the suggestion in itself. She is the communication (letter) herself. What she communicates is a matter of rousing irritation in the poet. It becomes a point of real irritation in the poet. The expression 'beneath the shimmer' is copiously suggestive of the trapping sinister intentionality of the 'Bella' or the beautiful woman. But, however, it is the next stanza that creates an equal amount of 'shimmer' or disturbance in the poet himself.

In the third stanza of the poem Ezekiel says:

> *Then I look at her. . .*
> *the colour disappears,*
> *she's short, thin dark*
> *without a cage to her name,*
> *as low as she can go.*[22]

First the poet saw her 'as colour only'. When he looked at her next 'the colour disappeared'. The subtle distinction that he makes in the act of 'seeing and looking' needs no explanation. Looking is always more concerned then seeing. The concern of the poet is equally obvious. He does not see her any more as a mere colour. She metamorphosis into a surprise or wonder born of the poet's concern for the object of his visitation. But his sense of surprise becomes highly irritating, when he consigns and comprehends in himself that:

> *She doesn't glance at me,*
> *waiting for her*
> *hawker or mill-worker*
> *coolie or bird-man*
> *fortuneteller,*
> *pavement man of medicine*
> *or street-barber on the move.*[23]

What all that goes in the name of poetry is the submission of his self-confounded comprehensions. Quite self-confoundedly the poet concieves that she was not glancing at him; and in waiting for all sorts of lovers who are the creatures like 'hawker' or 'mill-worker', etc. What if she is waiting for a poet like himself to comprehend rightly? But the poet's wrong apprehension shows his irritation rather than his concern. Such experiences are common place. Equally common place in men, their desires to be attended or devoted highly. But the objects as the things in themselves, always assumes' upon themselves a rare sense of inexcusability and inconclusiveness as our 'bella' on the road. It is a matter of the vanity of human wishes that the human beings, as heroic as they feel in themselves, nature the formed desires that the world of things should be readily available for their complete understanding. But the things in themselves always tease quite unendingly. The reference to the 'Bella' is merely a poetic device. The device is poetically situational.

But the real desire of the poet is in expression his irritation or for his comprehension. Therefore, Ezekiel sums up his meaning in the last stanza:

> *I see her image now*
> *as through a telescope*
> *without a single*
> *desperate moral*
> *to keep it in focus,*
> *remote and close-up.*
> *Of what use then to see and think?*
> *I cannot even say I carc or do not care;*
> *perhaps is a kind of despaired.*[24]

In stating 'I see her image now' the poet arrives at a rare conclusion that the things are inexhaustible in being what they are. First, he saw her as 'colour' only and now he 'sees' her as an image. It makes no big difference, until and unless you 'look' at her with a concern; and she pays equally concerned glances at you. But, unfortunately this never happens in the act of experiencing the things of the world. The existential manner of things is finely illustrated by Ezekiel by way of symbolizing the things in themselves in the artifice of 'bella'. But, however, the very desire to understand is a perinial force of being inhuman. Whether one understands or not the telescopic is in given for man. One should not bother for 'a single desperate moral to keep in focus'. In a very resigned manner he arrives at a momentary depression (again a poetic gesture of despondency), when he interogates 'what use then to see and think?'

He answers in a very emotional manner 'I cannot even say I care or don't care'. The word 'care' is synonymous with care. Care is the etymological origin of cure as a word. But, Ezekiel is concerned here with the word 'care' as a property of human concern. The ultimate realization of human limitations makes him dramatically utter 'perhaps it is a kind of despair'. Man not only wants to understand but also wants understanding in accordance with his own desires and fancies. The nature, to the extent that the human beings are also part of it, does not bother to give pride of place for human in the context of the created things of nature, that she (Nature) 'bella' waits for all the lower species and not for the poet himself is a created idea of the human beings. It has no validity in the true metaphysics of the things. Ezekiel's anxiety emerges out of his own dramatic conception that the bella was not waiting for him or was not paying a glance at him. This is what modern psychologists called ship-child-complex, where the child somehow come into the world, in spite of all the family planning precaution taken up by the parents. Man is such a step child to the extent that he starts exacting for a greater care and concern of himself by nature. On the other hand, the nature, like that bella who does not even glanced at the poet, always shows man his relative place in the nature of things in the world. Such a state of realization is really a matter of despair. This philosophical despair is the real theme of Ezekiel in many of his poems.

The Ability to Pursue New Resemblances

In the manner of inspired romantic, Ezekiel says that poets do not compose poems but poems are found, 'the best poet waits for words'. If we put a categorical question where such poems are found are the purpose of perceiving new resemblances through new metaphors, the answer lies that it is always in the poetic culture which a poet establishes by way of involving himself with the other poets. In this context Ezekiel to a great extent gets isolated from the Indo-Anglian poetic traditions that have been heavily relevant upon Indian language poetries. To that extent his departure from the Indo-Anglian traditions is obvious. Between 1948 and 1952 he lived in England and this brought him into contact with the new European trends of poetry in English. His poetry can be compared with that of the poets writing in England since the thirties, i.e. T.S. Eliot, W.H. Auden, W.B. Yeats, William MacNeice and Ted Hughes. They put upon his work a sort of inalienable influences. But, at the same time the new existential philosophy and the phenomenological approach, which were raging high during this period, enriched his way of thinking. The new movement poets, who established a clear existential approach to poetry, like William Carlos William and Wallace Stevens are of a great formative influences upon Ezekiel. In his prelude to 'Something to Pursue' Ezekiel clearly states:

That I may see myself
No longer unresolved,
But definite as mornings.[25]

This tendency of seeing himself 'no longer unresolved' is what he clearly emulated from Wallace Stevens and William Carlos William. It was William Carlos William who said that 'No ideas but in things'[26] this philosophy of contending with things around for the purpose of personal clarity is clearly existential. William Carlos William himself borrowed this poetic philosophy of things from Wallace Stevens who shared his goal of writing a poetry of things rather than ideas. The existential learnings of Ezekiel were copiously hinted by M. Garman when he said that 'the making of poetry out of existence is the highest synthesis possible and what Ezekiel declares him-self to be aiming at'. But, however, M. Garman did not elaborate the point as to where from Ezekiel acquired this poetic attitude. There are innumerable poems of Ezekiel which can be substantiated as intelligent analogies of the individual poems of his European and American poetical masters. There is a way of interpreting Ezekiel's *On Bellasis Road* to William Carlos William's *The Young House wife.* Ezekiel's *On the Bellasis Road* has been clearly explicated above. It is sufficient to hint at the analogical aspects of his poem with that of William Carlos William. William's poem is very short and goes as follows:

At ten a.m. the young housewife
moves about in negligee behind

the wooden walles of her husband's house.
I pass solitary in my car.

Then again she came to the curb
to call the ice-man, fishman, and stands
shy, uncorseted, tucking in
stray ends of hair, and I compare her
to a fallen leaf.

The noiseless wheels of my car
rush with a crackling sound over
dried leaves as I bow and pass smiling.[27]

Indian Poetry: An Analogy

Poetry for Nissim Ezekiel is an intellectual passion, a civilized man's cultivation coupled with choice of human concerns and cares. Very often it is an analogy for something that suddenly happens in the interior phenomena of his personality in a moment of raport with great art as formulated by the Western traditions. These moments of raports' are not limited to Western poetry alone. Western sculpture, West painting and even Western music to a certain extent invited his attention in one form or the other. His very association with Western culture is a matter of an objective intellectual passion rather than a blind and blinkered devotion towards what is sudden done in the European countries. He is discreet and discriminate in watering the Western forms of art and culture. In his heart of hearts he always maintained the rare love and passion for whatever it can be called, i.e. the Indian spirit. In the essay 'Naipaul's India and Mine' Ezekiel expresses his thoughts as follows:

> *I am not a Hindu and my background makes me a natural outsider: circumstances and decisions relate me to India. In other countries I am a foreigner. In India I am an Indian. When I was eighteen a friend asked me what my ambition was. I said with the naive modesty of youth, 'To do something for India'.*[28]

But then India and Indianism of his dream is certainly not that dogmatic and blind devotion to the Indian past.

This is not to say that Ezekiel is a great poet because he slavishly followed the modern Western poets. The greatness of Ezekiel as a poet lies in substantiating these influencial forces in order to comprehend the Indian cultural context and situations. In this sense he is a pure city poet, i.e. a Bombaywala making poetry out of his passionate personal experiences in Bombay and its subuerbs. His Bombay does not merely limit itself to the cosmopolitan population that inhabit that great city. His Bombay constitutes all the traditional, as well as the modern (post-Independence) institutions that turned that city into a rare mechanical and industrial centre. The people that inhabit Bombay invariably, but non-conspicuously, bear upon themselves the proud egocentricies that went to make that city. In short the properties of mechnization, urbanization, technocritization and civilization award an inevitable mark of identity of a modern city to Bombay. Dr. Srinivasa Iyengar rightly observes as follows:

> *The recurring note in Ezekiel's recent poems is the hurt that urban civilization inflicts on modern man, dehumanizing him, and subjecting his verities to pollution and devaluation. What is offered is dead-sea*

fruit, what we confront is the Medusastare.[29]

The expressions like 'dead-sea fruit' and the 'Medusastare' are significant here. Both his images speak of the carniv/orous state of the modern civilization. It is his *A Morning Walk* that he gives us the horrible pictures of Bombay life. Says Ezekiel:

Barbaric city sick with slums,
Deprived of seasons, blessed with rains,
Its hawkers, beggars, iron-linged,
Processions led by frantic drums
A million purgatorial lanes,
And child like masses, many tongued,
Whose wages are in words and crumbs.[30]

After undergoing the rigors of the vistas of Bombay his protagonist in the poem, i.e. the poet himself, nurtures himself a desire to escape from the modern squalor, at least imaginative. Says Ezekiel:

after the pain of his fragmented view
too late and small his insights came.[31]

These 'insights' even though they are imaginary, are equally true of human existence. Now 'his will is like the morning dew',[32] and he envisions a golden dream. Says Ezekiel:

The garden on the hill is cool
Its hedges cut to look like birds
Or mythic beasts are still asleep.[33]

This manner of a casual Bombay wala's nightmare turning into a pleasant dream is probably the authentic phenomena of an average Bombayite life. This kind of shift from nightmares to dream and then again from dreams to nightmares significantly evokes the fact that Ezekiel is not altogether dead to the enchanting positivities of life in its widesperad generality and charity. Therefore, he fervently prays in his *Morning Prayer* :

> *Whatever the enigma,*
> *The passion of the blood,*
> *Grant me the metaphor*
> *To make it human good.*[34]

This kind of passion for positive good in life comes to his from two different sources, one is the ancient traditional India of 'cool hills' and 'mythic beasts', the other sources which is obviously traceable to the influence of the British romantics, whose energetic imagination culminates into the grand poetry of W. B. Yeats. While Yeats runs to 'The Isles of Innesfree', Ezekiel true to the poetic genious of Yeats runs to the 'cool hills'. This kind of running to the 'cool hills' is unthinkable in the British romantic poetry for the obvious reasons that England is a cold country. India on the other hand is a tropical country where hill stations are the most common abodes of romantic escape, as well as of tourist interest. What exactly links Ezekiel with the Western romantics is to be found in the 'garden'. Ezekiel talking of the 'garden' on the 'hill' is slightly in acknowledged, but that is the influence of T.S. Eliot on Nissim Ezekiel.

REFERENCES

1. Nissim Ezekiel, *Hymns in Darkness* (Delhi: Oxford University Press, 1976), p. 9.

2. *Ibid.*
3. *Ibid.*
4. *Ibid.*
5. *Ibid.*
6. Hari Mohan Prasad and Chakardhar Prasad Singh, *Indian Poetry in English* (New Delhi: Sterling Publication Pvt. Ltd., 1985), p. 76.
7. *Ibid.*, pp. 76-77.
8. G.S. Balarama Gupta, ed., *The Journal of Indian Writing in English*, Vol. VII, (July 1979), p. 48.
9. Saleem Peeradina, ed., *Contemporary Indian Poetry in English: An Assessment and Selection* (Delhi: Macmillan, 1972), p. 12.
10. *Ibid.*
11. Unpublished thesis of Dr. S.B.K. Murthy, *Wallace Stevens and Existentialism* (Pt. Ravishanker Shukla University, Raipur, M.P.), 1979, p. 21.
12. Saleem Peeradina, ed., *Contemporary Indian Poetry in English: An Assessment and Selection* (Delhi: Macmillan, 1972), p. 12.
13. Michael Roberts, ed., *The Faber Books of Modern Verse* (London: Faber and Faber, 1965), p. 104.
14. Inder Nath Kher., ed., *Journal* of *South Asian Literature*, Vol. XI, Nos. 3-4 (Spring, Summer 1976), 1. 209.
15. Nissim Ezekiel, *Sixty Poems* (Bombay: Ekveera Press 1953), Preface.
16. *Ibid.*
17. Inder Nath Kher, ed., *Journal of South Asian Literature*, Vol. XI, Nos. 3-4 (Spring, Summer 1976), p. 17.
18. William Empson, *Seven Types of Ambiguities* (Penguin Book Ltd., 1971), p. 28.
19. Inder Nath Kher, ed., *Journal of South Asian Literature*, Vol. XI, Nos. 3-4 (Spring, Summer 1976), p. 209.
20. *Ibid.*, p. 210.
21. Nissim Ezekiel, *Hymns in Darkness* (Delhi: Oxford University Press, 1976), p. 22.
22. *Ibid.*
23. *Ibid.*

24. *Ibid.*
25. Inder Nath Kher, ed., *Journal of South Asian Literature,* Vol. XI, Nos. 3-4 (Spring, Summer 1976), p. 221.
26. Nina Baym, ed., *The Norton Anthology of American Literature* (New York: W.W. Norton & Co., 1986), p. 1756.
27. *Ibid.*, p. 258.
28. Inder Nath Khef, ed., *Journal of South Asian Uterature,* Vol. XI, Nos. 3-4 (Spring, Summer 1976), p. 203.
29. Dr. K.R.S. Iyengar, *Indian Writing in English* (New Delhi Sterling Publishers Pvt. Ltd., 1983), p. 660.
30. Nissim Ezekiel, *Latter-Day Psalms* (Delhi: Oxford Universtiy Press, 1982), p. 60.
31. *IbId,* p. 61.
32. *Ibid.*
33. *Ibid.*
34. Inder Nath Kher, ed., *Journal of South Asian Literature,* Vol. XI, Nos. 3-4 (Spring, Summer 1976), p. 65.

Bibliography

PRIMARY SOURCES

Ezekiel, Nissim. *A Time to Change and Other Poems.* London: Fortune Press, 1952.

Ezekiel, Nissim. *Sixty Poems.* Bombay: Ekveera Printers, 1953.

Ezekiel, Nissim. *The Third.* Bombay: The Strand Bookshop 1959.

Ezekiel, Nissim. *The Unfinished Man.* Calcutta: Writer's Workshop, 1960.

Ezekiel, Nissim. *The Exact Name.* Calcutta: Writer's Workshop, 1965.

Ezekiel, Nissim. *Hymns in Darkness.* Delhi: Oxford University Press, 1976.

Ezekiel, Nissim. *Latter-Day Psalms.* Delhi: Oxford University Press, 1982.

Ezekiel, Nissim. *Three Plays.* Calcutta: Writers Workshop, 1969.

Ezekiel, Nissim. 'Song of Deprivation'. *Enact,* July, 1969.

Ezekiel, Nissim. 'At Glance at USA'. *Littcrit.* Vol. 6, No. 1, June 1980, 1-7.

Ezekiel, Nissim. 'American Poet and Critic Today: An Indian Point of View'. *The Indian P.E.N.,* Vol. 44, Nos. 11-12, Nov.-Dec. 1978, pp. 1-11.

Ezekiel, Nissim. 'Don't Call it Suicide'. *The Bombay Literary Review,* No.1, 1989, pp. 99-120.

Ezekiel, Nissim. 'Indian English Poems of Bombay Poets', *Indian Literature,* Vol. 30, No. 4, Jul-Aug. 1987, pp. 135-36.

Ezekiel, Nissim. 'Marriage Poem', *The Literary Half-Yearly,* Vol. 10, No. 1, January, 1969, pp. 99-130.

Ezekiel, Nissim. 'What is Indian about Indo-English Poetry'. *Osmania Journal of English Studies,* Vol. 19, 1983, pp. 49-58

Fzekiel, Nissim. 'A New Arrival in Indo-Anglian Poetry', *Times Weekly,* Vol. 1, No. 29, 1971, p. 11.

Ezekiel, Nissim. 'Ideas and Modern Poetry', *Indian Writers in Conference.* The Sixth P.E.N. All India Writers' Conference Mysore, 1962.

Ezekiel Nissim (ed.), Bombay: The P.E.N. All India Centre, 1964.

Ezekiel, Nissim. 'Isn't Criticism Subjective', *The Times* of *India,* Dec. 28, 1975, 12.

Ezekiel, Nissim. 'The Knowledge of Dead Secrets—On the Wisdom of Sir Henry Harcourt Reilly' P. Lal (ed.), *T.S. Eliot—A Homage from India.* Calcutta: Writers Workshop, 1965.

Ezekiel, Nissim. 'Poetry and Philosophy—A Note', *Quest,* 50, Jul-Sept., 1966, 25-30.

Ezekiel, Nissim. 'Introduction', *Books Abroad,* Autumn, 1969.

Ezekiel, Nissim. 'Replies to Questionaire', *Modem Indian Poetry in English: An Anthology and Credo.* Calcutta: Writers Workshop, 1971.

Ezekiel, Nissim. 'K.N. Daruwalla', *Quest,* 74, Jan-Feb., 1972. 43-48.

Ezekiel, Nissim. 'Poetry as Knowledge', *Quest,* 76, May-June, 1972. 43-48.

Ezekiel, Nissim. 'Sri Aurobindo on Poetry', *Times* of *India.* Sunday, July 22, 1972.

Ezekiel, Nissim. 'Should Poetry be Read to Audiences', *The Sunday Statesman Magazine,* Aug. 27, 1972.

Ezekiel, Nissim. 'Naipaul's India and Mine', *New Writing in India.* London: Penguin, 1974.

SECONDARY SOURCES

Abidi, S.Z.H. *Studies in Indo-Anglian Poetry.* Bareilly: Prakash Book Depot, 1979.

Alphonso-Karkalam, J.B. *Indo-English Litereture in the 19th Century 1970.*

Amanuddin, Syed. 'Love and Sex in Indo-English Poetry', *Creative Moment.* Vol. III, No.1, Spring, 1974.

Ameeruddin, Syed. 'Trends in Indian Verse in English',

Commonwealth Quarterly. Vol. I, No. 4, Sept., 1977, pp. 1-13

Ameeruddin, Syed. (ed.). *Indian Verse in English: A Contemporary Anthology*. Madras: Poet Press India, 1976.

Bandyopadhyaya, P. (ed.). *The Voice of the Indian Poets*. Calcutta: United Writers, 1975.

Belliappa, Meena. 'Poet, Lover & Birdwatcher: An Explication', *The Miscellany*, 1971, pp. 25-44.

Beston, John B. 'An Interview with Nissim Ezekiel', *World Literature Written in English*, Vol. 16, No. 1., April, 1977, pp. 87-94.

Bhatia, H.S. (ed.). *Modern Trends in Indo-Anglian Poetry*. Delhi: Sita Publishers, 1982.

Bhatnagar, O.P. *Studies in Indian Poetry in English*. Amravati : Popular Book Centre, 1981.

Bhatnagar, O.P. 'The Indian Poetry in English: The Contemporary Situation', *The Literary Endeavour*, Vol. I, No. 4, April 1980, pp. 67-77.

Bhatnagar, O. P. & Vikramraj Urs (ed.). *New Dimensions in Indo-English Poetry*. Mysore : Commonwealth Quaterly, 1980.

Bhatnagar, O.P. (ed.). *Rising Columns: Some Indian Poets in English*. Amaravati : Kala Publication.

Bhatnagar, O.P. 'The Indian Poetry in English: The Contemporary Situation', *The Literary Endeavour*, Vol. I, No.4, April 1980. pp. 67-77.

Birbal Singh, Frank. 'An Interview with Nissim Ezekiel'. *Journal of South Asian Literature*, Vol. 22, No. 2, Sum-Fal 1987, pp. 130-38.

Birbal Singh, Frank. 'An Interview with Nissim Ezekiel'. *The Indian Literary Review*, Vol. 1 , No.10, Feb. 1979, pp. 2-8.

Bhatt, Gayatri. 'New Generation Poets: An Interview with Nissim Ezekiel'. *The Book Review*, Vol. 17, No. 12, Dec. 1993, p. 21.

Birje-Patil, J. 'Interior Cadences: The Poetry of Nissim Ezekiel', *The Literary Criterion*, Vol. 12, Nos. 2-3; 1976, pp. 198-212.

Bose, Amalendu. 'Some Poets of the Writers Workshop', *Critical Essays on Indian Writing in English*, ed. M.K. Naik,. Dharwar : Karnatak Univ., 1968.

Central Institute of India. A *Bibliography of Indian English*, 1972.

Chatterji, Suniti Kumar. *The Languages and Literatures of Modern India,* 1963.

Chida, A.R. (ed.). *An Anthology of Indo-Anglian Verse,* 1935.

Chida, A.R. (ed.). *Concise Encyclopaedia of English and American Poets and Poetry,* 1963.

Chaturvedi, P. D. 'New Poetry in India', *Commonwealth* Quarterly, Vol. 1, No. 5, Dec., 1977, pp. 41-52.

Coppola, Carlo. 'Nissim Ezekiel: The Most Recent Poems,' *The Commonwealth in Canada.* Parameswaran (ed.). Calcutta: A Writers Workshop Pub., 1983.

Dani, N.D. 'An Interview with Nissim Ezekiel'. *The Journal of Indian Writing in English,* Vol. 14, No. 2, July 1986. pp. 17-21.

Das, B.K. 'The Pattern of Thought in Poet, Lover & Birdwatcher:' *The Journal* of *Indian Writing in English,* Vol. 7, No. 2, July 1979, 46-48.

Das, Bijay Kumar. 'The Poetry of Nissim Ezekiel', *Modern Indo-English Poetry.* Bareilly : Prakash Book Depot, 1982.

Das, Bijay Kumar 'The Poetry of Nissim Ezekiel', *Contemporary Indo-English Poetry.* Bareilly : Prakash Book Depot, 1986.

Daruwalla, Keki N. (ed.). *Two Decades of Indian Poetry: 1960-1980.* New Delhi: Vikas, 1980.

Deshpande, Gauri. (ed.). 'Foreword', *An Anthology* of *Indo-English Poetry.* New Delhi: Orient Paperbacks.

De Souza, Eunice. 'Interviews with Four Indian English Poets'. *The Bombay Literary Review* No. 1, 1989. pp. 71-84.

Deswani, Tillotama. 'Review of 'The Exact Name,' *The Indian PE.N.,* 5 XXXII, May, 1966, 179-182.

Dutta, Ujjala. 'Problem of Sex, Self and Art in Nissim Ezekiel's 'Nudes', *Cygnus,* Vol. 2, No.1, 1980. pp. 49-57.

Dwivedi, A.N. (ed.). *Indian Poetry in English: An Anthology and A Literary History.* New Delhi· Arnold Heinemann, 1980.

Dwivedi, A.N. 'Nissim Ezekiel' Biography', *Indo-Anglian Poetry.* Allahabad: Kitab Mahal, 1979.

Dwivedi, A.N. 'Nissim Ezekiel': The Poetic Harvest', *Indo-Anglian Poetry.* Allahabad: Kitab Mahal, 1979.

Dwivedi, A.N. 'Imagery in Nissim Ezekiel's' Later Poetry', *Papers on Indian Writing in English:* Volumn. Poetry. Delhi: Amar Prakashan, 1991.

Dwivedi, A.N. 'Nissim Ezekiel: Nissim Ezekiel as a Poet', *Indo-Anglian Poetry.* Allahabad: Kitab Mahal, 1979.

Elango, N. *Poetry* as a *Record of Life: A Study on Nissim Ezekiel.* Tiruchirapalli : Dept. of English, Bharatidasan University, 1986.

Fraizer, R. W. *Literary History of India,* 1898.

Garman, Michael. 'Nissim Ezekiel-Pilgrimage and Myth', *Critical Essays on Indian Writing in English.* M.K. Naik et al. (ed.), Dharwar Karnataka University Press, 1972.

Garman, Micheal. 'Nissim Ezekiel-Pilgrimage and Myth', *Critical Essays on Indian Writing in English* Naik, M.K., S.K. Desai and G.S. Amur (eds.), Madras: The Macmillan Company of India, 1968.

Ghose, Lotika. *Indian Writers* of *English Verse,* 1933.

Gokak, V.K. *English in India: Its Present and Future.* 1964.

Gokak, V.K. (ed.). *The Literatures in the Indian Language.* 1954.

Gokak, V.K. & Inamdar, V.M. Compilers *Indian Classics in English Translation: A Short Bibliography,* 1956.

Goodwin, Gwendoline. *The Anthology* of *Modern Indian Poetry.* 1927.

Gowda, H.H. Anniah. 'Refin'd with the Accents that are Ours': Some Reflections on Modern English Poetry in India, Africa and the West Indies', The Colonial and the Neo-Colonial *Encounters in Commonwealth* Literature. Mysore: University of Mysore, 1983.

Gokak, V.K. (ed.). *The Golden Treasury* of *Indo-Anglian Poetry:* 1828-1965. New Delhi: Sahitya Akadmi, 1970.

Gokak, V.K. (ed.). *Twenty-one Indo-Anglian Poems.* New Delhi: Sahitya Akademi, 1975.

Guruprasad, Thakur. 'Nissim Ezekiel's 'Enterprise', Indian *Scholar,* Vol. 3, No.1, Jan. 1981, pp. 13-18.

Harrex, S.C. 'A Critical Approach to Indo-English Poetry', *Only Connect: Literary Perspectives East and West.* Amirthanayagam Guy and S. C. Harrex (eds.). Adelaide: Centre for Research in the New Literature in English and East-West Center, 1981.

Hess, Linda. 'Post-Independence Indian Poetry in English', *Quest,* 49, April-June, 1966, 30-34.

Hess, Linda. 'Post-Independence Indian Poetry in English', *Consideration.* Mukherjee Meenakshi (ed.). New Delhi: Allied Publishers Pvt. Ltd., 1977.

Iredale, Roger. 'Indian Poetry in English Today', *Quest* No. 98, Nov.-Dec., 1975, pp. 73-74.

Iyengar, K.R. Srinivasa. 'The New Poets', *Indian Writing in English.* New Delhi: Sterling Publishers Pvt. Ltd., 1972.

Iyengar, K.R. Srinivasa. 'Review of 'The Unfinished Man.' *The Indian PE.N.,* XXVII, March 31, 1961, 109-110.

Iyer, Shashl 'America Through the Eyes of a Poet'. *Span.* 4. XVII, April 1976, 29-32.

Iyengar, K.R. Srinivasa. 'The New Poets', *Indian Writing in English.* New Delhi: Sterling Publishers Pvt. Ltd., 1962.

Iyengar, K.R. Srinivasa. *Indo-Anglian Literature,* 1943.

Iyengar, K.R. Srinivasa. *The Indian Contribution to English Literature,* 1945.

Iyengar, K.R. Srinivasa. *Two Cheers for the Commonwealth: Talks on Literature and Education,* 1969.

Iyengar, K.R. Srinivasa and Nandakumar Prema. *An Introduction to the Study* of *English Literature,* 1966.

Jaggi, S. D. 'Indo-English Poetry in the Context of World Poetry', *Minimix,* Summer 1975.

Jussawalla, Adil. 'The New Poetry', *Reading in Commonwealth Literature. Walsh William* (ed.), Oxford: Clarendon Press, 1973.

Kalinnikove, Eleana J. 'New Poetry', *Indian English Literature.* A *Perspective.* Sharma K.K. (ed.), Ghaziabad : Vimal Prakashan, 1982.

Kabraji, Fredoon. *This Strange Adventure: An Anthology of Poems of English by Indians:* 1828-1946, 1967.

Karnani, Chetan. 'The Poetry of Nissirn Ezekiel: A Brief Overview', *Journal of South Asian Literature.* Vol. XI, Nos. 2-3, 1976. 223-28.

Karnani, Chetan. *'Introduction',* Nissim Ezekiel, New Delhi: Arnold Heinemann, 1974.

Karnani, Chetan. 'IOA Time to Change', *Nissim Ezekiel.* New Delhi: Arnold Heinemann, 1974.

Karnani, Chetan. 'Introduction', *Nisslm Ezekiel,* New Delhi Arnold Heinemann, 1974.

Karnani, Chetan. 'Sixty Poems', *Nissim Ezekiel.* New Delhi, Arnold Heinemann, 1974.

Karnani, Chetan. 'The Unfinished Man', *Nissim Ezekiel.* New Delhi: Arnold Heinmann, 1974.

Karnani, Chetan. 'The Exact Name', *Nissim Ezekiel.* New Delhi: Arnold Heinemann, 1974.

Karnani, Chetan. 'A Very Indian Poet in Indian English', *Nissim Ezekiel.* New Delhi: Arnold Heinemann, 1974.

Karnani, Chetan. 'Three Plays', *Nissim Ezekiel.* New Delhi: Arnold Heinemann, 1974.

Karnani, Chetan. 'Literary and Art Criticism', *Nissim Ezekiel.* New Delhi : Arnold Heinemann, 1974.

Karnani, Chetan. 'Ezekiel's Recent Verse', *Nissim Ezekiel.* New Delhi: Arnold Heinemann, 1974.

Karnani, Chetan. 'Achievement of Nissim Ezekiel', *Nissim Ezekiel.* New Delhi: Arnold Heinemann, 1974.

Karnani, Chetan. 'Bibliography', *Nissim Ezekiel.* New Delhi. Arnold Heinemann, 1974.

Kasture, P.S. 'The Nature of Chaos in Modern Indo-Anglian *Poetry', Recent Commonwealth Literature',* Vol. II. Dhawan, R.K., P.V. Dhamija and A.K. Shrivastava (eds.), New Delhi: Prestige Books, 1989.

Kher, Inder Nath. 'That Message from Another Shore. The Aesthetic Vision of Nissim Ezekiel', *Contemporary* Indian English Verse: An Evaluation. Chirantan Kulshrestha (ed.), New Delhi: Arnold Heinemann, 1980.

King, Bruce. 'Ezekiel and His Influence', *Modern Indian Poetry in English.* New Delhi: Oxford Univ. Press, 1987.

King, Bruce. 'The Poet's India I : Ezekiel, Ramanujan, Patel, Daruwalla, Shiv Kumar', *Modern Indian Poetry in English.* New Delhi: Oxford Univ. Press, 1987.

King, Bruce. 'Nissim Ezekiel: 1948-1965', *Three Indian Poets: Nissim Ezekiel. AK. Ramanujan and Dom Moraes.* Madras: Oxford Univ. Press, 1991.

King, Bruce. 'Ezekiel: Later Poems', Three Indian Poets: Nissim

Ezekiel', *Contemporary Indian Poetry in English*. New Delhi: Atlantic Publishers and Distributors, 1991.

Kurup, P.K.J. 'Voyage: The Self in the Poetry of Nissim Ezekiel', *Contemporary Indian Poetry in English*. New Delhi: Atlantic Publishers and Distributors, 1991.

Kher, Inder Nath. 'That Message from Another Shore: The Aesthetic Vision of Nissim Ezekiel', *Mahfil*, Vol. 8, No. 4, 1972, 17-28.

Kher, Inder Nath. 'Guest Editor', *Journal of South Asian Literature*, Nissim Ezekiel Issue, Nos. 3-4, XI, Spring, 1976.

Kohli, Devindra. 'Passionate Sincerity in Indian Poetry in English', *Journal of Commonwealth Literature*, Vol. 9, No. 1, Aug. 1974, pp. 10-19.

Kohli, Suresh. 'Nissim Ezekiel: Pursuit of Perfection', *Indian and Foreign Review*. Vol. 8, No. 14, 1971, pp. 18-19.

Kumar, Shiv K. 'Poster Prayers of Nissim Ezekiel' Defiant Questioning in Recent Poems', *Journal* of *South Asian Literature*, Vol. XI, Nos. 3-4 Spring, Summer 1976, 263-64.

Kotoky, P.C. *Indo-English Poetry*, 1969.

Kumar, Shiv K. (ed.). *Indian Verse in English:* 1970. New Delhi: Writers Workshop, 1971.

Lal, P. 'An Arrival in Indo-Anglian Poetry', *The Alien Insiders: Essays on Indian Writing in English*. Calcutta: A Writers Workshop Book, 1987.

Lall, Emmanuel Narendra. 'Nissim Ezekiel: Images of Woman', *The Poetry* of *Encounter: Three Indo-Anglian Poets:* D. Moraes, AK. Ramanujan, N. Ezekiel. New Delhi: Sterling Pubs. Pvt. Ltd., 1983.

Lal, P. Rao, Raghuvendra K. (ed.). 'Introduction', *Modern Indo-Anglian Poetry*. New Delhi: Kavita Pubs., 1959.

Lahiri, K.C (ed.). *Indo-English Poetry in Bengal*. Calcutta. Writers Workshop, 1974.

Lal, P. (ed.) *Modern Indian Poetry in English: An Anthology and* a *Credo*, 1969.

Lal, P. & K.R. Rao, eds. *Modern Indo-Anglian Poetry*, 1960.

Mallik, Keshav. 'Review of Hymns in Darkness', *Youth Times*, March 18-31, 1971, p. 53.

McCutchion, David. 'Examen de Midi', *The Miscellany,* 29, Oct. 1968, pp. 71-73.

Misra, Soubhagya. 'Ezekiel: An Estimation', *Graybook* ' Spring, 1972, 18-27.

Mohanty, Niranjan. 'The Home-Bound Pilgrim A Study of Nissim Ezekiel's Poetry', *The Rajasthan Journal of English Studies,* Nos. 13-14, 1981, pp. 161-76.

Macleod, A.L. (ed.). *The Commonwealth PEN: An Introduction to the Uterature of the British Commonwealth,* 1961.

McCutuchion, David, *Indian Writing in English: Critical* Essay. 1968.

Mehta, Digish. 'A Search for a Perspective: *Nissim Ezekiel's Background*

Casually' ', *Indian English Literature: Since Independence.* Paniker K. Ayyappa (ed.) New Delhi: The Indian Association for English Studies, 1991.

Mehta, P. P. 'Nissim Ezekiel', *Contemporary Indo-English Verse Vol. I A Collection of Critical Essays on Male Poets.* Dwivedi A.N. (ed.). Bareilly: Prakash Book Depot, 1984.

Naik, M.K. and Others (eds.). *Critical Essays on Indian Writing in English,* 1968.

Naik M K. and others (eds.) *Indian Response to Poetry in English:* Essays in Honour of V.K. Gokak.

Naik, Pritish (ed.). *Indian Poetry in English:* 1947-1972 – *An Anthology,* 1972.

Narasimhaiah, C.D. (ed.). *Indian Literature of the Past Fifty Years:* 1917-1967, 1970.

Narasimhaiah, C.D. (ed.). *The Swan and the Eagle,* 1969. Jawaharlal Nehru. *The Discovery of India,* 1946.

Nandy, Pritish (ed.). *Indian-English Poetry in Bengal,* 1947-1972. New Delhi: Oxford, 1972.

Nandy, Pritish (ed.). 'Introduction'. *Modern India1 Poetry.* New Delhi: Arnold Heinemann Pub. 1974.

Nandy, Pritish (ed.). 'Introduction', *Indian Poetry in English Today,* New Delhi: Sterling Pub. Pvt. Ltd., 1973.

Nagarajan, S. 'Nissim Ezekiel', *Contemporary Poets* (ed.), James Vinson. New York: St. Martins Press, Second edition, 1975. 1231-32.

Nandkumar, Prema. 'Annual Survey of Indian Wirting in English', *The Indian Literature.* 4, XIII, 1970, 35-36.

Nandy, Pritish. 'Indian Poetry in English: The Dynamics of a New Sensibility', *Indian Literature,* Vol. 14, No.1, 1971, 8-12.

Nabar, Vrinda. 'Domesticity and Drama: An Analysis of Nissim Ezekiel's Marriage Poem and Don't Call it Suicide', Contemporary Indian Drama. Pandey, S. & F. Taraporewala (eds.) New Delhi: Prestige Book, 1990.

Naik, M.K. 'The Tale is in the Sting: An Analysis of Nissim Ezekiel's 'Night of the Scorpion', *Dimensions* of *Indian English Literature.* New Delhi: Sterling Pub. Pvt. Ltd. 1984.

Nandy, Pritish. 'Introduction', *Indian Poetry in English Today.* New Delhi : Sterling Publishers Pvt. Ltd. 1973.

Nandy, Pritish. 'Introduction', *Modern Indian Poetry.* New Delhi: Arnold Heinemann, 1974.

Narayan, Shyamala A 'Nissim Ezekiel's Latter-Day Psalms: A Stuty', *Contemporary Indo-English Poetry.* B.K. Das (ed.), Bareilly: Prakash Book Depot, 1986.

Oaten. E.F.N *Anglo-Indian Literature,* 1908.

O'Donnell, Margaret J. (ed.). *An Anthology of Commonwealth Verse.* 1963.

O'Donnell, Margaret J. (ed.). *An Anthology of Commonwealth Verse.* London: Blackie and Son, 1963.

P.E.N. All India Centre. *Writers in Free India,* 1949.

Pandey, N.B. (ed.). A *Book of India: An Anthology of Prose and Poetry from the Indian Subcontinent,* 1965.

Parthasarathy, R. (ed.). *Ten Twentieth Century Indian Poets.* Delhi: Oxford Univ, Press, 1976.

Peeradina, Saleem. (ed.). *Contemporary Indian Poetry in English: An Assessment and Selection.* Bombay: Macmillan, 1972.

Padhi, Bibhu. 'The Parallel Voice: A Study of the New English Poetry in India', *Quest,* No. 98, Nov.-Dec., 1975, pp. 39-46.

Paniker, K. Ayyappa. 'Four Voices and a Medium', *Indian Book Chronicle,* Vol. 2. No. 11, June 1, 1977, 190-91.

Parthasarathy, R. 'Foregrounding as an Interpretative Device in Nissim Ezekiel's I Night of the Scorpion', *The Literary Criterion,* Vol. 10. No. 3, 1974, pp. 38-44.

Peeradina, Saleem (ed.) *Contemporary Indian Poetry in English.* Bombay : Macmillan, 1972.

Panikar, K. Ayyappa. 'Beyond Irony: The Third Vision of Nissim Ezekiel', *Indian Literature in English.* Madras: Anu Chithra Pub., 1989.

Parthasarathy, R. 'Indian English Verse: The Making of a Tradition'. *Alien Voice: Perspectives on Commonwealth Literature.* S. Avadhesh K. (ed.). Lucknow: Print House Pub., 1981.

Parthasarathy, R. (ed.). 'Introduction', *Ten Twentieth Century Indian Poets.* Oxford University Press, 1976.

Patke, Rajeev S. 'Canons and Canon-making in Indian Poetry in English', *From Commonwealth to Post-Colonial.* Rutherford Anna (ed.) Sydney: Dangaroo Press, 1992.

Prasad, S. N. 'The Cognitive Self in Nissim Ezekiel: An Approach to His Poetry', *Indian English Literature: Since Independence.* Paniker K. Ayyappa (ed.), New Delhi: The Indian Asso. for Eng. Studies, 1991.

Prasad, Hari Mohan. 'Frontiers of Indian Poetry in English: A Study in Culture, Language, and Tradition', *Indian Poetry in English,* (ed.) H.M. Prasad, Aurangabad : Parimal, 1983.

Prasad, H.M. & Singh, C.P. (eds.). *Indian Poetry in English.* New Delhi: Sterling Pubs., 1985.

Raghunandan, Lakshmi. 'Nissim Ezekiel', *Contemporary Indian Poetry in English.* New Delhi: Reliance Publishing House, 1990.

Rahman, Anisur. 'Objective Form in Nissim Ezekiel', *Form and Value in the Poetry of Nissim Ezekiel.* New Delhi: Abhinav Pub., 1981.

Rahman, Anisur. 'Images and Symbols', *Form and Value in the Poetry of Nissim Ezekiel.* New Delhi: Abhinav Pubs., 1981.

Rahman, Anisur. 'Poetry is Another Rhythm', *Form and Value in the Poetry of Nissim Ezekiel,* New Delhi: Abhinav Pubs., 1981.

Rahman, Anisur, 'Select Bibliography', *Form and Value in the Poetry of Nissim Ezekiel,* New Delhi: Abhinav Publication, 1981.

Rahman, Anisur. 'Technique and Motif in Nissim Ezekiel's

Three Plays', *Indian Writing in English.* Sinha Krishna Nanda (ed.), New Delhi: Heritage Publishers, 1979.

Raizada, Harish 'Nissim Ezekiel's Poetry of Love and Sex', *Living Indian English Poets.* P. Madhusadan (ed.), New Delhi: Sterling Publishers Pvt. Ltd., 1989.

Ram, Atma. 'Academics as Poets: A Viewpoint', *Indian Poetry and Fiction in English,* New Delhi: Bahri Publications, 1991.

Rao, K. Raghuvendra. 'The Alienation Games: The Poetry of Nissim Ezekiel', *Perspectives on Indian Poetry in English.* Naik, M.K. (ed.), New Delhi: Abhinav Publications, 1984.

Reddy, P. Bayapa. 'The Poet as Dramatist: Nissim Ezekiel Interviewed', *Studies in Indian Writing in English.* New Delhi: Prestige Books, 1990.

Rao, R. Raj. 'Themes of Alienation in Nissim Ezekiel's Plays', *Contemporary Indian Drama.* S. Pandy & T. Freya (eds.), New Delhi : Prestige Books, 1990.

Reddy, P Bayapa. 'Minor Joys and Sorrows: Ezekiel's Marriage Poem', *Studies in Indian Writing in English,* New Delhi: Prestige Books, 1990.

Reddy, P. Bayapa. 'The Hollowness of the Middle Class Society: Nalini', *Studies in Indian Writing in English,* New Delhi: Prestige Books, 1990.

Rao, Raghavendra. 'The Alienation Games: The Poetry of Nissim Ezekiel', *Perspectives on Indian Poetry in English,* (ed.) M.K. Naik, 98-108.

Roger, Irendele. 'Indian Poetry in English Today'. *Quest.* 98, Jan.-March. 1966, pp. 72-74.

Rose, Paul d'Gama 'So Much Light in Total Darkness', Review of Hymns in Darkness, *Kavi,* Jan., 1975, pp. 32-35.

Sahitya Akademi. *Contemporary Indian Literature: A Symposium.* 1959, Sahitya Akademi, *Who's Who of Indian Writers,* 1961.

Sahitya Akademi. *Bibliography* of *Indian Literature, 20th Century,* Vol. I, 1962.

Santhanam, K. (ed.). *An Anthology of Indian Literature,* 1970.

Seshadri, P. *Anglo-Indian Poetry,* 1930.

Sett, Adi K. (ed.) *An Anthology of Modern Indian Poetry,* 1929.

Singh, R.P.N. (ed.), A *Book* of *English Verse on Indian Soil,* 1966.

E. E. Speight (ed.) *Indian Masters of English*, 1934.

Saha, Subhas Chandra, 'Review of 'The Unfinished Man', *Thought*, 40, XXI. Dec., 1969, pp. 16-18.

Saha, Subhas Chandra. 'Enterprise', *Insights*. Calcutta: Writers Workshop, 1972.

Sergeant, Howard. 'Poetry of the Commonwealth', *English*, Vol. XV, No. 90, Autumn 1965.

Shahane, Vasant A. 'The Religious-Philosophical Strain in Nissim Ezekiel's Poetry', *Journal of South Asian Literature*, Vol. XI, Nos. 3-4, 1976, 253-61.

Singh, Satyanarayan. 'Ramanujan and Ezekiel', *Osmania Journal of English Studies*, 1, 1969, pp. 67-75.

Singh, Satyanarayan, 'Journey into Self: Nissim Ezekiel's Recent Poetry', *Osmania Journal of English Studies*, Vol. 13, No.1, 1977, pp. 29-43.

Sivaramkrishna, M. 'New Poetry in India', *The Times of India*, March 6, 1977.

Sivaramkrishna, M. 'No Longer an Adjunct', *Review of Hymns in Darkness, Indian Book Chronicle*, 7, II, April, 1977, 123.

Sivaramkrishna, M. 'Contemporary Indian Poetry in English: An Approach', *Opinion Literary Quarterly*, Vol. I, No. 4, July, 1974, pp. 39-57.

Srinath, C.N. 'Review of 'The Exact Name' ', *The Literary Criterion* 3, *VII, Winter*, 1966, pp. 87-89.

Srinath, C.N. 'Contemporary Indian Poverty in English', *The Literary Criterion*, 2 VIII, Summer, 1968, pp. 56-58.

Srivastave, Avadhesh K. 'New Voices : Diversions on Recent Indo-Anglian Poetry', *Indian Writing in English*, ed. K.N. Sinha, New Delhi, Heritage Pubs., 1979, pp. 109-127.

Sergeant, Howard. (ed.) *Pergamon Poets 9 : Poets from India-N. Ezekiel, A.K. Ramanujan, R. Parthasarathy, O.K. Das'*. Oxford: Pergamon Press, 1970.

Saha, Subhas C. (ed.). *An Anthology of Indo-English Love Poetry*. Calcutta: Prayer Books, 1976.

Sinha, R.P.N. (ed.). *A Book of English Verse on Indian Soil*. Bombay: Orient Longmans, 1996.

Saha, Subhas C. 'Enterprise', *Insights*. Calcutta: A Writers

Workshop Publication, 1972.

Sharma, S.D. 'Rebellious Mood: Nissim Ezekiel', *Thematic Dichotomy of Writings in Indian English. Indology and Culture.* Bareilly : Prakash Book Depot, 1985.

Shanane, V.A. & Sivaram Krishna, M. (eds.). *Indian Poetry in English: A Critical Assessment,* New Delhi: Macmillan, 1980.

Sinha, Krishna Nandan. (ed.). *Indian Writing in English,* Delhi' Heritage Publishers, 1979.

Sinha, R.P.N. *The Birth and Development of Indo-English Verse.* New Delhi: Dev Publishing House, 1971.

Singh, Frankbirbal. 'My Being Human: An Interview with Nissim Ezekiel', *Contemporary Indian-English Poetry.* Ram, Atma (ed.) Calcutta: A Writers Workshop Pub., 1989.

Singh, Satyanarain. 'Journey into Self: Nissim Ezekiel's Recent Poetry', *Indian Poetry in English: A Critical Assessment.* Shahane, V.S. & M. Sivaramakrishna (eds.). India: The Macmillan Ltd., 1980.

Singh, Satyanarain. 'Ramanujan and Ezekiel', *Contemporary Indian English Verse: An Evaluation.* C.Kulshrestha (ed.), New Delhi: Arnold Heinemann, 1980.

Sreenivasan, S. 'The Self and its Enchanted Circle: A Perspective on the Poetry of Nissim Ezekiel', *Changing Traditions in Indian English Literature* Rajan. P.K. (ed.). New Delhi: Creative Books, 1995.

Suka, V. *A Thematic Study of Nissim Ezekiel's Poetry.* Madras: Dept. of English, Madras Christian College, 1986.

Syal, Pushpinder. 'Indianness in Style and Discourse: Nissim Ezekiel's 'The Railway Clerk and Night of the Scorpion'', Structure *and Style in Commonwealth Literature,* New Delhi: Vikas Publishing House Pvt. Ltd. 1994.

Taranath, Rajeev. 'Ezekiel's Nalini', *Indian Drama.* Mysore: Prasaranga, 1974.

Taranath, Rajeev and Meena Belliappa. *The Poetry* of *Nissim Ezekiel* Calcutta: A Writers Workshop, 1966.

Tonetto, Walter and Enrique Martinez 'Nissim Ezekiel: Inlets to an Indian Sensibility', *Australian and Indian Literature.* New Delhi: Indian Society for Commonwealth Studies, 1991.

Taranath, Rajeev. 'Nissim Ezekiel', *Quest,* 74, Jan.-Feb., 1972.

Taranath, Rajeev and Belliappa, Meena. 'Nissim Ezekiel's Poetry' *Miscellany*, No. 19, 1966, 47-65.

Verghese, C. Paul. *Problems of the Indian Creative Writers in English*, 1971.

Verghese, C. Paul. 'The Poetry of Nissim Ezekiel', *Indian Literature*, IXV, March, 1972, pp. 73-75.

Verghese, C. Paul. 'Indian Poetry in English Today: An Assessment'. *The Indian PE.N.* ,Vol. 40, Nos. 2-3, Feb-March, 1974, pp. 1-6.

Verma, K.D. 'Myth and Imagery in 'The Unfinished Man': A Critical Reading', *Journal of South Asian Literature.* Vol. XI, Spnng, Summer 1976, 229-239.

Verghese, C. Paul. 'The New Poetry', *Problems of the Indian Creative Writer in English.* Bombay: Somaiya Publications Pvt. Ltd., 1971.

Walsh, William, 'Two Indian Poets', *The Literary Criterion*, 3. II, Winter, 1974, pp. 1-16.

Walsh, William, 'Small Observations On a large Subject', *Aspects of Indian Writing in English*, (ed.) M.K. Naik, Madras: Macmillan, 1979, 101-119.

Wieland, James. 'Making Light of the Process: Nissim Ezekiel's Poetic Fictions', *Indian Poetry in English*, ed. H.M. Prasad. Aurangabad : Parimal, 1983.

Wieland, James. 'The Development of Technique in the Poetry of Nissim Ezekiel', *Journal of South Asian Literature*, Vol. XI, Nos. 3-4, Spring, Summer 1976, pp. 241-52.

Walsh, William. 'The Meeting of Language and Literature and the Indian Example', *Writers in East-West Encounter: New Cultural Bearings.* A. Guy (ed.) London: Macmillan, 1982.

Walsh, William. 'Poetry: Ezekiel, Parthasarathy, Kolatkar, Ramanujan and other', *Indian Literature in English.* Carroll David and Michael Wheeler (eds.) U.S.A.: Longman, 1990.

Walsh, William. 'Small Observations On a Large Subject', Aspects of *Indian Writing in English* M.K. Naik (ed.) Madras: The Macmillan Company of India Ltd., 1979.

Walsh, William. 'The Indian Sensibility in English', *Awakened Conscience: Commonwealth Literature. Narasimhaiah*, C.D. (ed.), New Delhi: Sterling Publishers, 1978.

Wieland, James. 'Making Light of the Process: Nissim Ezekiel's Poetic Fictions', *Indian Poetry in English.* H.M. Prasad (ed.) Aurangabad : Parimal Prakashan, 1983.

Williams, H.M. *Indo-Anglian Literature.* Bombay: Orient Longman, 1976. Wiseman, Christopher. 'The Development of Technique in the Poetry of Nissim Ezekiel', *Contemporary Indian English Verse: An Evaluation.* K. Chirantan (ed.), New Delhi: Arnold Heinemann, 1980.

Wiseman, Christopher. 'The Development of Technique in the Poetry of Nissim Ezekiel: From Formality to Informality', *Considerations.* M. Mukherjee (ed.), New Delhi: Allied Publishers Pvt. Ltd., 1977.

Index